The Writing Habit

OTHER BOOKS BY DAVID HUDDLE

A David Huddle Reader: Selected Prose and Poetry

Short Stories

A Dream with No Stump Roots in It
Only the Little Bone
The High Spirits
Intimates

Poetry

Paper Boy
Stopping by Home
The Nature of Yearning

The

Writing

Habit

David Huddle

UNIVERSITY OF VERMONT
Published by University Press of New England
Hanover and London

UNIVERSITY OF VERMONT
Published by University Press of New England,
Hanover, NH 03755

Originally published as a Peregrine Smith Book
by Gibbs Smith, Publisher

Printed in the United States of America
5 4 3 2

CIP data appear at the end of the book

ACKNOWLEDGMENTS: "The Writing Habit" appeared in *1989 Novel & Short Story Writer's Market.* "Memory's Power" appeared in *Creativity and the Writing Process and 1987 Fiction Writer's Market.* "Issues of Character" appeared in *Mid-American Review.* "Let's Say You Wrote Badly" appeared in *The New York Times Book Review, The Bread Loaf Anthology of Contemporary American Essays,* and *1990 Novel & Short Story Writer's Market.* "Puttering in the Prose Garden" appeared in *Green Mountains Review and 1988 Fiction Writer's Market.* "Taking What You Need" appeared in *Writers on Writing: A Bread Loaf Anthology and Writer's Craft/Teacher's Art: Teaching What We Know as Writers.* "Story Truth" appeared in *The New York Times Book Review and The Writer.* "What You Get for Good Writing" appeared in *1992 Novel & Story Writer's Market.*

For Ghita Orth and Barbara Murphy

Contents

The Writing Habit

1 THE WRITING HABIT

the major difficulty a writer must face has nothing to do with language: it is finding or making the circumstances that make writing possible. The first project for a writer is that of constructing a writing life.

Achievement in writing requires many hours and many pages of concentrated effort. That work must be carried out in a sustained fashion: a writer must be able to carry what has been learned from one day's writing into the next, from one week's writing into the next, and so on. Significant accomplishment in writing depends on growth. A writer's development depends on being able to write regularly and without distraction.

The actual details of writing lives differ with the personalities of individual writers. I remember a lecture given by the novelist Don Bredes, a very down-to-earth man, in which he set forth what he thought were the requirements of a writing circumstance. Shelves, he said, were necessary, in order to set out one's manuscripts, supplies, and reference materials. A phone immediately at hand was necessary so that one would not be ripped away from one's desk when the phone rang in another part of the house. A window with a view was necessary, but I don't remember if Don thought one's desk should face toward the window or away from it. And a plant, preferably a cactus, was necessary. I haven't remembered why Don thought one needed a plant—probably something to do with the benign influence of a low-profile living presence.

In her memoir of her father, Susan Cheever describes the young John Cheever putting on a suit and tie each morning, riding the elevator down to a basement storage room of their Manhattan apartment building, taking off his trousers and hanging them up with his coat to prevent wrinkling, and in his boxer shorts sitting down to his writing desk for his day's work. The established Cheever claimed to have written each of his later books in a different room of his Ossining, New York, home.

Eleanor Ross Taylor has written an intriguing description of the poet Randall Jarrell, apparently a very sociable man, keeping a writing pad and pen with him in his home, and writing intermittently all through his day, while entertaining visitors and tending to domestic duties.

I have had various writing circumstances, some of them refined to a state of high peculiarity. The most productive of them came together in the winter of 1978 when I lived alone in a cottage beside a small lake. I rose at sun-up, did fifteen minutes of calisthenics, showered, made coffee and ate a light breakfast. Then I worked at "fresh" writing, beginning around seven or seven-thirty. I tried not to excuse myself before eleven, though if momentum was with me, it was o.k. to stay later. My output for those hours was three to six pages of fresh prose each morning. I composed on a portable electric typewriter, the humming of which always seemed to me like very good company. I used canary yellow "second sheets" for that first draft material. My desk faced a large window that overlooked a woodsy hillside where I had set out bird food. For some reason I took to lighting a large "patio lantern" candle when I sat down to work and to blowing it out when I felt I had finished for the morning.

Those months of living beside Lake St. Clair were the one period of my life when I have been a runner, or more accurately a jogger. My run was my reward for having worked through my morning hours. Just as I had had to work up to my three or four hours of fresh writing a day, I had gradually to increase my running distance. The road around Lake St. Clair is a very hilly 2.3 miles long. When I began running in early February, I could trot only about a quarter of the way around it without stopping to walk—and I would always walk the rest of the way around, often picking up my pace again after I'd caught my breath. When I left Lake St. Clair in mid-May I was jogging (vigorously) around it twice without stopping. On the run I occasionally saw a pileated woodpecker, a blue heron, wild turkeys, and various other birds.

When I returned from jogging, I did some stretching, took a shower, and fixed myself a light lunch. For the first time in the day, I listened to the radio; I neither read, nor was I tempted to read, any newspapers during my lakeside tenure. After washing my lunch and breakfast dishes, I was in my "free period." I could do whatever I wanted. Whatever I wanted was almost always to read for a while and then to take a nap.

A few words here about naps: I'm convinced that naps are an essential part of a writing life, that they "clean" the brain by discharging the clutter and allowing the subconscious to address some of the central issues of the morning's writing. If I know I want to do some more writing in the afternoon, I'll always try to schedule that session immediately after a nap. It's rare for me to try to accomplish fresh writing in the afternoon, but I often try to carry out revisions if I have at least an hour or more of afternoon time available to me.

When I woke from a nap at Lake St. Clair, I had the delicious sensation of having nothing pressing to do and not having to hurry with whatever I chose to do. Most often I simply lay in bed, letting my mind wander as it would. Because I had minimum distraction there, whatever I was writing was what I thought about most of the time. It wasn't long after I awaked from my nap that I would turn to my manuscript; usually I'd be curious about the pages I'd written that morning and want to check them out. Of course, as I read, I reached for a pen to make corrections, changes, notes, and it wasn't uncommon for me to find myself again sitting before the typewriter, relighting my candle, retyping the morning's pages, perhaps even proceeding into a page of "fresh writing" without consciously deciding to do so. These afternoon writing sessions usually lasted only an hour or two, but I always considered them a bonus. Because my writing days became so productive, I felt more and more virtuous while I lived at Lake St. Clair.

At the end of an afternoon work session, I rewarded myself with a walk around the lake. I made myself walk slowly and try to observe my surroundings as carefully as I could. The world itself seemed especially charged with energy; it became an intense presence in my life. I was primarily interested in birds—I'd bought a field guide and begun keeping a list of the birds I saw— but I also became a student of the landscape, the variety and quality of light in different weathers and at different times of day. I suspect that the attention I paid to the world of my 2.3 mile walks around Lake St. Clair was of benefit to me in my writing. The fiction I wrote during those months seems to me informed by the world's presence and to articulate an intense connection between my characters and the world around them.

In the evenings I listened to the radio—jazz or classical music. Sometimes I worked on my writing. Evening work sessions were rare and likely to come about only if I was trying to complete a finished draft of a story and what had to be done was merely typing clean copy. Mostly I read, because reading had become unusually exciting to me: I felt as if I were reading on two levels, for the usual pleasure of poetry and narrative and also for my writerly education. In the works of other authors, I was able to observe technical achievement that I thought would be of eventual use in my own work.

I got sleepy early. It was rare that I didn't turn out my bedside light by ten or ten thirty. I went to sleep thinking about the writing I'd accomplished and about the work I meant to do the next morning. The telephone did ring now and then, and I had visitors, visitors I wanted and ones I didn't want. But what I had most of the time at Lake St. Clair was solitude, which instructed me: the more of it I had, the more I learned to make use of it. When a writing life is in good order, as mine was then, everything is relevant to it; every detail of one's day has a connection to one's writing.

I have been a resident of artists' colonies at Yaddo and the Virginia Center for the Creative Arts; on some occasions I have been able to work better at those places than at home, but in my best colony experience I've been only about fifty percent as productive as I was at Lake St. Clair. The obvious difference is that colonies have a social life that I felt I had to attend; I was guaranteed solitude during the day, but in the evenings I ate with the other colonists, I chatted after dinner, I made friends, and so on. This social life can be a healthy influence in a writing life, especially if two writers begin exchanging manuscripts and criticism. Along with valuable friendship, a writer can also find inspiration and illumination from visual artists and composers. But finally a social life is a distraction. Instead of having the evening hours to compose yourself, to let your mind wander back to the writing, you become involved with others. In the morning, when there should be no obstacles between self and work, you find you're reviewing last night's conversation.

Lake St. Clair was a temporary situation for me brought about by the luckily converging circumstances of a sabbatical leave from teaching at the University of Vermont, an NEA Fellowship that paid the bills for it, and a wife who for those months was willing to look after herself and our daughter. I have often wondered how different things would have been if I had thought of it as my permanent circumstance. Would all that solitude have seemed so luxurious then, or would it have seemed a punishment, a burden, an entrapment? Would I have found my work so fulfilling if I had believed it must take the place of my family? I don't think my writing would be helped by being permanently without the company of family and friends. Most likely I was able to put my solitude to such excellent use because I knew there would be an end to it.

When I left the lake, I had come to think of myself as a kind of esthetic saint. I had lost weight. I was in excellent physical condition. I had stripped my life down to what was essential to me. I had accomplished a greater quantity and a higher quality of writing than I ever had before. I had established a meaningful connection between myself and the natural world. I felt this exhilarating rightness to my life. I felt certain that I would be able to transport the habits I had formed into my "regular life," which now (from my saintly viewpoint) seemed cluttered, distracting, piggish, physically and esthetically unhealthy.

The disintegration took about a week. If I did my early morning calisthenics anywhere in the house, I made such a clatter that I woke my wife and daughter. My wife had to go to work and my daughter had to go to day-care; their preparations necessarily disturbed my concentration on my work. Near my house there was nowhere to run or walk without encountering traffic and carbon monoxide. In the house, everywhere I looked, there were little chores that needed doing, dishes to be washed, toys to be picked up, stacks of magazines to straighten, bills to pay, a screen with a hole in it, a borrowed book that needed to be returned. The phone rang more often now that I was back in my own community. I played tennis, I met a friend for lunch, I attended a surprise birthday party. I snacked between meals. I watched TV. In short, I drifted away from my writing life. My Lake St. Clair habits were not transportable.

Before and after my tenure at Lake St. Clair, I was a sporadic writer—if I had something I was working on, I worked at it until I finished it; then I didn't write again until something else pressed me urgently enough to begin it and pursue it. For periods of as long as a year, I wrote nothing. I had a rationale worked out about being a sporadic writer: I wasn't a factory, and it was only because of a national assembly-line mentality that American writers felt obligated to churn out books. Who needed another piece of writing anyway? If I wasn't writing, it probably meant I had nothing worthwhile to say. And so on. But my Lake St. Clair experience demonstrated to me what it felt like to have a real writing life, to have something that held my attention over a period of time, to have ongoing, deeply fulfilling work. I have never been able to duplicate that experience, but because I had it that once, it gave me something to aspire to again. I've gotten better and better at constructing a writing life for myself in the midst of my "regular life." I don't have any remarkable secrets about it, but I do have what I think are a few useful concepts.

To write well one must use one's "good hours" for one's writing. My good hours are the first three or four of my day. If I want to use them for my writing, that means I have to get up early and start writing before other demands are made on me. A few people I know have their good hours late at night, and that's when they should be writing. A poet I know warms up slowly; she finds her good hours to begin around mid- or late-morning.

Since I teach school for a living and since much of the work of my teaching involves reading and responding to student manuscripts, I find that I have to use my "next-best hours" (late morning or afternoons) for that work. But responding to student manuscripts is almost always in direct competition with my own writing for my good hours; I have to be clever to manage a heavy teaching load with a productive writing schedule. On a day when I teach my first class at 9:25 and I have a dozen student stories to respond to, I'll need to get up at 4:00, be at the writing desk by

4:45, work on my own writing until 6:00, write my responses until
8:30, and get to my office by 9:15.

Along with using my good hours for my writing, I've learned
more about how to use my less-good hours for clearing the way for
efficient use of my writing time. I'm a house-husband, which means
that I have cooking, laundry, cleaning, and child-care duties to
attend to, and like most writers I am very distractable; house-hus-
banding can devour my good writing hours if I let it. But nowadays
my motto is that everything has to get done sometime, and the trick
is to make sure that my writing always comes first. Taking a break
from my writing, I can wash the dishes because doing that little
task is just distracting enough to give me a new "take" on whatever
it is I'm working on Putting away laundry can often be a very useful fifteen-minute writing break. I can pay my bills while my printer
is typing up a manuscript. What I understand better and better is
how to clear the way to my good hours with my writing. Before I go
to bed I try to have my little computer, with its battery charged,
waiting for me, preferably with the document I'm working on ready
to come up on the screen when I switch it on. I want my reading
glasses right where I can find them, my coffee thermos clean, and
the room straightened up. If I have bills to pay or letters that need
to be answered, I want them neatly stashed where they won't catch
my eye first thing when I sit down to write.

Robert Hass's poem "Measure" uses the phrase "the peace of
the writing desk." These words accurately describe my own experience. My writing time is when I set my life in order. I examine
my life through the act of writing. Although I try to sell most of
my writing, my first desire for it is that it be as truthful and beautiful as I can make it out of what I know and think and feel.
Therefore writing is to me a kind of meditation. It isn't a purely
spiritual activity, but it is one in which my spirit is nourished.
Writing has become so essential for my daily life that I feel
denied if I miss a day of "the peace of the writing desk."

When I tell people that I get up at 4:30 or 5:00 to do my writing, they often praise my discipline, but now that my writing life has been established, discipline has nothing to do with it. Getting up to do my writing requires no more discipline than sitting down to eat a meal or going to bed at night to get some sleep. It's natural and necessary.

Flux has never been an easy principle for me to understand or to incorporate into my life. My make-up is conservative. My instinctive way of doing things is to try to get them just right and then to keep them that way. Some nasty lessons have taught me that I had better give flux its due. Thus it was silly of me to try to import my Lake St. Clair writing habits into the life I lived in my home with my family. Instead of becoming frustrated because I couldn't repeat my successful methods, a more intelligent course of action would have been to try to discover the different writing habits that would work in that different situation.

Cheever needed different rooms of his house because at different times of his life, he was a different writer and was writing different books. Learning to understand and monitor one's own writerly needs is the main project of a writer's education. Beginning writers almost always feel that they have to learn the secrets that all successful writers have mastered. They think they need to take possession of something outside themselves. Writing teachers are often frustrated because they can't make students see how they're looking away from the place where the real secrets are located. The elements of a writer's making are within the individual, and they are different with each individual. Each writer makes his own habit.

I write well at 5:30 a.m. sitting in an easy chair with a portable computer in my lap, a coffee thermos and a cup by my chair, and Glenn Gould playing Bach's "Well-Tempered Klavier" on the stereo. Across town, a little later, Alan Broughton will be sitting at his desk in his study using a pencil and a legal pad for his first draft, which he will later in the day type into his word processor because he can't read his handwriting if he lets it sit "untranslated" more than a few hours. And even later, between classes, in his office at St. Michael's College, John Engels will be furiously annotating the manuscript of a poem he printed out yesterday. He will completely dismantle and reassemble his poem in the minutes available to him between conversations with students and colleagues who drop by to see him.

The options are various. If you're a would-be writer, what you need to find out is not how someone else works but how you are inclined to work. You have to determine your good hours, the writing tools and the writing environment that best suit you, the limitations you can overcome and the best methods for dealing with the limitations you can't overcome.

You also have to become aware of your inclinations toward laziness, dishonesty, glibness, and other personal foibles. You have to become skillful at outwitting those negative aspects of your character. For instance, I know I am inclined to send manuscripts out before they're really ready to be submitted any place—before they're finished. I haven't been able to correct this failure, but I've gotten so I can delay my sending out a manuscript by giving copies of it to certain friends of mine to read and respond to it before I make up a "final copy." The more friends who give me responses to a manuscript, the more drafts I'll run it through. The help of peers is essential to most of the writers I know. To discuss our work, I meet with two other writers about every three weeks; we try to bring fresh writing or significant revisions to our meetings. We try to be very tough-minded in our responses to each other's work. Not only are these other two writers helpful to me as critics; they also inspire me to work regularly in hopes of producing something they will appreciate.

Like most writers, I'm a highly skilled procrastinator. I've had to develop the appropriate counter-skills. One of my more successful counter-procrastinating techniques is the bend-and-snap-back move: I'll tell myself yes, I really do need a break right now, but the only way I can justify it is by using it to accomplish some little task that might distract me from writing tomorrow morning.

These maneuvers of self against self for the good of getting my work done are not unlike similar moves I've learned for improving the writing itself. For instance, I have come to understand that I am weak when it comes to portraying female characters as whole human beings. My natural, porcine inclination is toward second-rate versions of characters like Hemingway's Maria, Faulkner's Eula Varner Snopes, Nabokov's Lolita, and Terry Southern's Candy. My more responsible writing self must always be questioning and arguing with this lesser Huddle. The tension is a healthy one for my writing; my female characters get so much of both the porcine and the responsible varieties of my attention, that in a few instances I've been able to create portraits of women who have both sexual force and emotional-intellectual complexity. And I count myself lucky that I'm able to write across gender even as well as I have been able to do so far.

Managing contraries within the self is an ability that must be cultivated by a writer, both in and out of the work. Your natural inclinations are often less than admirable, but rather than trying to eliminate them from your personality, you can learn how to change them into positive elements of your writing. Thus you can convert your inclination toward distraction and procrastination into habits that will clear the way toward using your good hours for concentrated writing. Thus you can transform your inclination toward fantasizing about wish-fulfilling female characters into the creation of appealingly whole human beings. Such alchemy is still possible in a well-constructed writing life.

Once you understand that your negative qualities can be put to use both inside and outside your writing, you can begin to be kind to yourself. No longer necessary are those lectures, "You lazy such and such, you took a nap when you should have been writing, you can't write about women, you sent out that story too soon, you..." Instead of flailing away like that, you can become crafty, learn how to use your whole self in your writing.

Hemingway had a rule that has been especially useful for my work. He thought you ought to stop writing for the day at a point where you knew what you were going to do next. I like that notion just as it stands—often at the end of my morning's writing session, I will make a few notes about what I think ought to come next. I also think a writer needs to stop work with a little bit of energy left. I feel good when I've written enough to be tired, but if I've written myself into a state of exhaustion, I don't feel so eager to get back to work the next day.

Hemingway's quitting-time axiom is one version of what seems to me a basic principle of the writing life: you must nourish the "ongoingness" of your work. Sometimes I convince myself that what is crucial is to finish this piece or that piece of writing, that the only thing that matters is to get this manuscript in the mail. But a real writing life is nothing so desperate as all that, not something you do merely for a day or a month or a year. Stories, poems, essays, and books are the by-product of a writing life; they are to be cherished, but they separate themselves from their creators and become the property of editors, reviewers, and readers. For a writer, the one truly valuable possession is the ongoing work—the writing habit, which may take some getting used to, but which soon becomes so natural as to be almost inevitable.

2 MEMORY'S POWER

I am sitting in a pick-up truck in Bowling Green, Ohio, with somebody I thought I respected a great deal, and this somebody is telling me that they liked Phil O'Connor's novel *Stealing Home* pretty well until they got to know Phil and his kids and their little league experience and all that, and then it didn't seem like the book was that much of an accomplishment, it was just the way it was for Phil, he didn't have to make up very much of it. I could have argued, but this person had just treated me to ham and eggs and homefries with coffee and the large tomato juice, and I was there in a truck in Bowling Green, where one direction is just about as good as another and it's too flat to argue with anybody, you need altitude, hills and valleys, rocks and crannies, and so on to have a good argument. So I gave this person the kind of look my photographer friend gave me when I told him once that I thought photography couldn't possibly be an art, all you had to do was take this little, ugly, black machine, point it somewhere and press a button, that's all there was to it, and what art was there in that?

But now I'm in Vermont, there's plenty of altitude available, and I can argue to my heart's content. Whether or not it's all right to write real stuff and call it fiction is the question. I do realize that there is an argument here: there are two sides to be put forth, and the other side often seems very attractive to me. I believed Ay

Kwai Armah when he said, in a workshop at Columbia, after a reading of a particularly charged piece of autobiographical fiction, that that kind of writing, was, for the author, like spending capital instead of spending interest: you'd run out of it soon, if you kept doing it.

John Irving seems to me persuasive when he says—and here I'm paraphrasing remarks I've heard him make in lectures, workshops, and conversations at Bread Loaf—that "because something actually happened is no reason whatsoever for including it in a fiction," when he says that purely autobiographical novelists usually have only one good book in them, and when he says that autobiographical writing often indicates a failure of the imagination.

And John Cheever could say just about anything he wanted to, and I'd be nodding my head, yes, yes, yes. Here Cheever is, in an interview in the *New York Times*, putting autobiography in its place:

> It seems to me that any confusion between autobiography and fiction is precisely the role that reality plays in a dream. As you dream your ship, you perhaps know the boat, but you're going towards a coast that is quite strange; you're wearing strange clothes, the language that is being spoken around you is a language you don't understand, but the woman on your left is your wife. It seems to me that this not capricious but quite mysterious union of fact and imagination one also finds in fiction. My favorite definition of fiction is Cocteau's: "Literature is a force of memory that we have not yet understood." It seems that in a book one finds gratifying, the writer is able to present the reader with a memory he has already possessed, but has not comprehended....

And that seems right to me, it makes me want to nod my head

when I read it, even though it's contrary to what I want to put forth here. A lot of good people have a lot of bad things to say about the use of autobiography in fiction, and they seem to lift their voices when they speak on this particular subject, as if they really feel strongly about it: keep autobiography out of fiction.

But my recent experience has been to write a book of autobiographical poems (which is o.k.; poets don't get as fired up on the subject as fiction writers do) and a sequence of six long autobiographical stories. I didn't start out writing that way. I began with made-up stories, probably for the same reason that most everybody does; I took the word fiction literally and wrote imagined stories, stories with made up characters and made-up events.

I feel a little bit guilty nowadays about my writing so autobiographically. So much so, in fact that I put a disclaimer in my book of poems that says, "These poems are fictions. The truth they attempt to achieve is personal and imaginative, not historical." What that amounts to is telling a lie that these true poems are lies. Well, some of them are. It gets complicated. I put that disclaimer in partly because I felt bad at having used—and that's the word that applies here, *used*—so much of what actually happened in my family and in the town where I grew up. But I also put it in because my wife's a lawyer and she assured me that some of the people in my poems, Pig Clemons, Jeep Alley, Deetum Dunford, Monkey, Dude, Hat, and Hitler Dunford, Phoenix Hill, Geronimo Spraker, and so on, might like to sue their old buddy David Huddle, haul him into a court of law. I can't quite feature being sued for something I put into a poem, but the idea makes me nervous. So I put my disclaimer in, and now I'm safe, if just a little guilty-feeling.

I'm also grateful, to autobiography, because I was given those poems and stories to write at a time when I had just about given up on myself as a story-writer. My made-up stories had become shorter, thinner, more fragile. I knew the next one I wrote was going to disappear right in front of me, it was going to unwrite itself as I took each page out of the typewriter. When I speak of autobiographical fiction here, I mean stories whose basic impulse comes out of memory. If the thing begins in memory, no matter how much made-up stuff is in it, I consider the story to be autobiographical.

The stories my students gave me in my first years of teaching were successful for various reasons, maybe a different reason for every story, and those reasons seemed to me only vaguely connected to anything I said or did in class, anything I allegedly taught. But when the stories were unsuccessful, they were unsuccessful for a few reasons that I could clearly and positively name:

◆ The unsuccessful stories were too abstract and not concrete enough. They were too much of the mind and not enough of the senses. About this, Wei T'ai, an eleventh century Chinese poet says, "Poetry presents the thing in order to convey the feeling. It should be precise about the thing and reticent about the feeling, for as soon as the mind responds and connects with the thing, the feeling shows in the words; this is how poetry enters deeply into us." Allen Tate, in *The Fathers*, says, "There is not an old man living who can recover the emotions of the past; he can only bring back the objects around which, secretly, the emotions have ordered themselves in memory." And Flannery O'Connor, to whom I am more than willing to give the last word says, "The beginning of human knowledge is through the senses, and the fiction writer begins where human perception begins." This abstract/concrete business is the main issue I deal with in my writing classes. At the end of every semester I am sick of hearing myself say the same thing about it that I said in the first classes. Like most of the crucial issues of story writing, it's a point that's so true and obvious there's no shock value in it.

◆ The unsuccessful stories were inadequately considered. Which is to say that the writer didn't work as hard as his story wanted him to. The writer did not hold the material in his mind and heart for an adequate amount of time. He did not bring all of his mental and emotional strength to the story. He did not revise enough. I am always telling my stories that I can finish them in three or four drafts, and they are always telling me that I can't finish them in fewer than seven or eight drafts. I have more than once told myself that if I had known how much work writing stories was going to be, I never would have gotten involved with it. Right this minute I have several unsuccessful stories of my own on my desk at home, and these mock me each time I look at them. "You did not give us enough," they say. "When will you come to us and give us everything?"

◆ Finally, the unsuccessful stories I received from my students were written by a false self. In most cases this false self is an overly literary fellow, a user of fancy diction and elaborate syntax, a manipulator of characters who are too good and beautiful for this world or else who are so thoroughly terrible and evil that a reader might keep his children indoors for days if he took them seriously, and these characters usually sit still, making grand speeches to each other or thinking profound thoughts to themselves until the right moment, when violence is called for. Thomas Williams writes about a writer of such stories in his novel, *The Hair of Harold Roux*; Harold Roux, who wears a wig, ignores his own history, of growing up in a coal town, in order to write about a pretty life he wishes he'd had among the rich and beautiful.

The reasons for writing out of a false self are various and complicated. Wish fulfillment may have a lot to do with it. Maybe we ought to be forgiven for writing wishfully, for presenting ourselves as much more heroic, intelligent, right-thinking, effectual, articulate, ecological, potent, and good-smelling than we actually are, But it is the way of good readers, the ones we really want, not to be forgiving of wish-fulfillment.

I have been reluctant to assign subjects to my students: write about a chase, a trip, a baby, an older person, somebody looking out a window, an argument, that sort of thing. It has seemed to me that choosing a subject is one of the few democratic aspects of an activity that I consider to be almost totalitarian in character. But in pondering these three reasons—and some others—for many of my students' turning out unsuccessful stories, I hit upon the notion of restricting them to autobiographical material as a way of directing them to potentially better stories. For a summer school course, I made up a questionnaire that forced students to explore just about all the memory they had available to them. You'd be surprised how many of us feel that our own lives are not literarily worthy, our lives are just not interesting enough, we'd have to write about somebody else. My questionnaire demonstrated to all of us that we did have material to write about, we didn't have to be so humble about our dumb, boring lives, Writers who try exploring their own histories are often surprised at what happens. A good many people would say, "I can't remember all those things. It's too far back."

You do not, even those of you with very strong memories, remember whole chunks of your lives. You remember in small pieces, fragments, maybe just the way the light of a summer morning shown through the curtains of your bedroom when you first woke up one day thirty or forty years ago. But when you sit down to write, you discover that one thing leads to another, and that in the act of writing, you can recover many fragments of your life that have been lost to you; you can begin to recover whole chunks of your history. "It's all back there somewhere," one of my informed friends told me, tapping the back of his head. If you think about that bedroom curtain, you remember, of course, that your mother made it, that she made matching bedspreads for you and your brother, and that you would stand beside her sometimes while she worked, and you had to be quiet when she was peddling, and, and, and...

Memory and imagination are our only resources. Our stories are either remembered or imagined or—and this is most often the case—they are both remembered and imagined, they come out of a combining of the two resources. In both memory and imagination, one thing leads to another. I tell my classes that the most important decisions and discoveries in my own writing have occurred between one sentence and the next, between one paragraph and the next. During the two thwacks my thumb makes on the space bar after I've thunked down a period with the fourth finger of my right hand—during that little piece of space and time, I hope to receive, if only occasionally, the whole force of what we call "creativity," which may in fact be just the process of one thing leading to another, the energy of the imagination, the energy of memory. And that's probably the strongest argument I know for sitting down to the paper and getting on with it rather than going into the other room to pace and think and wait.

Stories that work soothe me. I remember them by way of details, scenes, sentences, dialogues. I remember them, I cherish them, I savor them over the years. I still grin to myself over the story that Judy Towne, a sophomore from Milton, Vermont, wrote for a class of mine several years ago, a story in which a girl and a boy meet at a party, leave and go down the hall to a dormitory room where they talk about cooking pizza, and in the conversation it becomes clear to them that romance is not possible for them. When stories don't work I forget them, everything in them, all the details. That's the ultimate form of literary revenge; it's what you do to a bad story instead of shooting it.

The story that doesn't work because it's overly abstract is usually the result of the beginning writer's misconception, his belief that his task is primarily intellectual and that he must be profound. Flannery O'Connor addresses the point forcefully when she says that "there's a certain grain of stupidity that the writer of fiction can hardly do without, and this is the quality of having to stare, of not getting the point at once." And Robertson Davies says that "All sorts of people expect writers to be intellectuals. Sometimes they are, but it is not necessary to their work.... I do not say that writers are childlike creatures of untutored genius; often they are intelligent people, but the best part of their intelligence is of the feeling and intuitive order."

I could tell my students in the beginning that you don't have to be smart to write well, which is certainly in large part true, but I expect they'd resist the notion. They're sitting in that classroom in the first place because, as they've probably been told many times, they have good minds. Most of us have been taught that it is a lot better to be smart than to be stupid. We are taught to respect intellect, and I suspect we are also taught disrespect for the senses. Usually when we think of how our senses come into use, we think of dope, loud music, drunkenness, eating too much.

So there is a kind of reversal of values that must take place for a writer to begin to write good, concrete stories. He must learn to respect the senses—Joseph Conrad advised us that "All art ... appeals primarily to the senses, and the artistic aim when expressing itself in written words must also make its appeal through the senses...." I believe that the beginning writer must learn at least some disrespect for the intellect, just enough disrespect to keep his mind from spoiling his material.

We may have been taught to intellectualize almost everything around us, but we remember our own lives in almost purely sensuous terms. In my classroom, I may get up on my academic high horse and begin to discourse on the fragmented existential universe suggested through exotic diction, erratic syntax, pessimistic humor, and cunningly random structure in the fictions of Donald Barthelme, but when I write, out of memory, of a summer morning in my early childhood, it goes like this:

Just at the foot of her front porch were her pink tea roses. My grandmother, in her white dress, her white stockings, the prim little black lace-up shoes, stood with her hand behind one of the small opening rosebuds. "Isn't this lovely?" she asked. She put her nose near the pink flower. It was the middle of a hot day. Her grey hair shone in the sunlight. The roses smelled sweet and hot, as if they were cooking.

My point here is simply that autobiographical writing leads us naturally toward concrete writing, toward language that involves the nose, tongue, ears, skin, and especially the eyes, as well as the mind.

A misconception is also responsible for the inadequately considered story. The notion here is that writers are clever devils, skillful manipulators of their audiences, primarily technicians. Out of this misconception come stories that may be mildly interesting but that are simply not felt, stories that lack conviction. Hayden Carruth, in *Harper's*, speaks exactly to this point when he says, "Let there be passion, along with talent.... Passionate vision, passionate concern: these make works of art." And John Irving, in *The Washington Post Book World,* is also speaking to the point when he says,

> I had a class of graduate-student writers once. Their favorite story—written by one of them—was a story about a three-course meal from the point of view of a fork. The fork was the main character. It was a very sophisticated piece of writing, and brilliantly funny. In the end, in an especially well written scene, the fork got thrown out in the trash. The only problem was: I wasn't sad about what happened to the fork. The entire experience of the story was intellectual. It was the best story I ever read about a poor fork—but I am not a fork, and I don't care what a fork feels.

For the writer who sees his job as primarily technical, one

thing is as good as another; a fork as subject matter is just as valid as the French Revolution, an asparagus patch just as powerful as an Ahab, a Sutpen, or a Gatsby. In fact it is this arbitrariness that is a primary virtue of "the new fiction." Donald Barthelme, a writer who's done some wonderful stories but whose work all too often lets me put it down before I've finished it, begins one of his *New Yorker* stories this way:

> When Captain Blood goes to sea, he locks the doors and windows of his house on Cow Island, personally. When Captain Blood, at sea, paces the deck, he usually paces the foredeck rather than the afterdeck—a matter of personal preference. He keeps marmalade and a spider monkey in his cabin, and four perukes on stands.

I see virtues of language and wit in such a paragraph, but when I have tried it out, I don't feel compelled to go on to the next paragraph. I feel that the objects in this paragraph—the afterdeck and the foredeck, the marmalade, the spider monkey, and the four perukes on stands—are like stuff the writer has thrown out of the back of a closet. If one thing is as good as any other thing, then nothing makes much difference, whatever the closet offers is good enough.

What I want in a story, and I suspect it is what most people want, is the quality of passion and of necessity. I don't want what the writer throws out of his closet onto the floor behind him; I want his best brandy, and I want him to take me to the special room where he keeps the thing in the house that he cares about the most, and I want him to tell me about it in such a way that I begin to care for that thing, too.

There are fine writers who achieve stories of passion and necessity wholly through the imagination. Kafka's "The Metamorphosis" is the shining example, and here are its first two sentences:

> As Gregor Samsa awoke one morning from uneasy

dreams he found himself transformed in his bed into a gigantic insect. He was lying on his hard, as if it were armor-plated, back and when he lifted his head a little he could see his dome-like brown belly divided into stiff arched segments on top of which the bed quilt could hardly keep in position and was about to slide off completely.

The first sentence might have given me some doubts about whether or not to go on, but the second, with its rigorous working out of the consequences of the first—if the man has turned into an insect and just awakened, then this must be what his first perceptions would be—is so urgently necessary that I feel that I must go on to the third, and so on.

But Kafka is exceptional. Most writers are, in my opinion, most passionate when they are working out of memory, or mostly out of memory. We will take liberties with made-up characters, made-up lives, but we become more responsible when we are dealing with our own lives and the lives of those people who are important to us. Complexity may have something to do with it. We know our own experience to have been enormously complicated, and if we are to write about it, we feel that we must catch something of the nature of that complication. We resist simplification. We resist the arbitrary. In our own lives, we know that things happened in a certain way, and those things were necessarily that way and not some other way. When we are using the material of our own history, we are most likely to find passion and to engage in that rigorous weighing and balancing of chance and choice, of surprise and inevitability, that the well-considered story requires of us. I believe that memory is the most likely route for a writer to follow in locating material about which he can write passionately and urgently; working through memory, we are most likely to avoid the arbitrary and to make connections in our stories that are necessary, inevitable, and meaningful. We may very well want to be surprised by a story as we are reading it. But when we have come to the end, and we are looking back at it, reflecting, we want to have a sense that what happened in that story was inevitable. We want to be able to say, yes, that's how it would have gone.

Memory operates by way of the senses, by way of detail, which is the stuff of fiction, the fabric of good stories. For me, memory serves as real stuff, material, matter, fabric, clay, bricks and mortar, lumber and nails, plaster, what have you. The use of memory makes the act of writing more craftsmanlike, if you will. Humbler. Tom Wolfe (speaking at the University of Michigan) said that "when you're in your late teens or early twenties and you want to write, you want to feel that the only thing that matters is your genius. The material, the content of the writer's work, is merely the clay, the wax, that Himself is going to use." I can remember feeling that way, but I can also remember feeling nervous about it, anxious, knowing even then, as I think everyone knows at any age, that talent is fragile, talent is luck, talent is given and so talent might be taken away at any time. Nowadays I know I am not the graceful magician who makes a story come into being, poof, out of thin air. I do hope to be the slow worker who drives the truck with a busted muffler and a back end that's got in it every kind of brick, pipe, board, wire, string, tool, scrap, and piece of something that I ever might need.

What can be said against trying to write autobiographical fiction? John Irving names two negative aspects with his phrase, "the tyranny and self-importance of autobiography in fiction."

By tyranny I understand him to mean the power that personal fact brings to bear on the writer. If we know that an event happened in a certain way, it is very difficult for us to change it, even though the esthetic requirements of our story might demand change. There is a kind of rigidness, or more accurately maybe, brittleness, about autobiographical material that might be described as tyranny. The writer who would use the material to make stories must be able to let go of what he knows to be historical truth, must be willing to lie and to revise that historical truth into imaginative truth.

By self-importance I understand John Irving to mean the writer who uses his writing to promote himself. It is true that autobiographical fiction writing can bring out the worst in anybody, the would-be celebrity who has just been waiting for a chance to tell the world about himself, the preacher-educator who wants to correct the deviant behavior of everyone else through the revelation of his own exemplary life, and so on. We are all of us, writers and non-writers, heroes, unrecognized heroes, of the stories we imagine ourselves to be living; everything we do or say is an effort to make the rest of the world conspire in our personal fictions, our personal protagonism. If we practice autobiography without rigorous self-judgment, which is the balancing opposite of self-importance, the result probably will be obnoxious.

Writing autobiographically involves not only revealing ourselves to the world—which although frightening is also a little bit thrilling—but also writing about others, our family-members, our friends, our enemies. Diplomatic relations can be strained. There can be a lot of trouble. I remember Peter Taylor's sheepish look when he told of his father meeting him at the airport once to tell Peter that if he'd been around when the father read that story that Peter'd published somewhere about Aunt-So-And-So, the father would have punched him in the face. I have a sickening memory of a telephone conversation I had with my parents just after they'd read a story of mine, about Vietnam, which was published in *Esquire* while my younger brother was stationed at Cam Ranh Bay. My own personal record is not exemplary, but in spite of my record, my obvious hypocrisy notwithstanding, I think I have good advice to offer: I believe the writer must do whatever he can to avoid such trouble, to keep from hurting feelings, but I believe finally he cannot allow the opinions and feelings of others to stop or to interfere with his writing. Maybe this is the ultimate selfishness, to say that one's own work is more important than the feeling of family and friends. Autobiographical writing will bring you to the point of having to make not just one but a number of hard choices between the life and the work.

Almost every semester in the classroom, I am asked the very good question: for whom do we write? I try to answer as loudly as I can and with no more than an instant's hesitation, "We write for ourselves first, and then we write for others." The question isn't an easy one, and my answer is more like a mantra for me—a formula I might say to myself over and over to give myself comfort. In story-writing there is always that torturous measuring of self and other: on the one hand I might be writing a story about this nincompoop husband, writing it with total disregard for what my real sister and brother-in-law think about me. And maybe that's admirable—more admirable if it's a good story than if it's a bad one. But I might also be writing the story so that my younger brother, the one my real sister was always tattling on, will love me better. Can I really ever say, I wrote this story for me and for no one else? Or for my younger brother, or the reader at the edge of the forest, for the fisherman out at dawn, for anybody anywhere, real or imagined? The more you worry that question, the more you have to back away from it to keep from falling into it. But I think there is a better answer than the one I've been offering. For whom do we write? We write for the work itself. We ourselves are devious, complicated, finally unknowable even to ourselves, and you others out there are devious and complicated and certainly unknowable to me. Experience washes over us and is gone forever. The world rushes at us and then rushes away from us, and as Country Joe and the Fish put it so succinctly, "Whoopee, we're all gonna die." We write for the work itself. Because the work stays. Because the work may very well be devious and complicated, but it is a rock, it will hold steady, it will be regarded, it is finally knowable.

In the first place we write for the work itself. In the second place we write for ourselves. And in the third place we write for others. This civilized ordering (work, self, others) does not ignore the reader, nor does it intrude upon the writer's own integrity. It simply puts first things first whether the writing comes from memory or from imagination, whether it uses fantasy or autobiography—and in this ecstasy of my conclusion the materials have come not to matter so much anymore—the first consideration is this, to make the thing beautiful. No matter who sees it.

APPENDIX:

Questionnaire for an Autobiographical Portrait:

1. Describe subject physically: face, hair, hands, feet, body, gestures, way of walking, voice, clothes, etc. What are subject's most pleasing physical characteristics? Most displeasing?

2. What are subject's habits? What patterns are there in his or her life?

3. Describe the landscape and the house, or apartment, or room where subject lives now. (Provide details of all appropriate sense impressions here.) Describe how subject lives in this environment.

4. Describe the behavior of subject outdoors, both during the day and at night. How does subject respond to seasonal changes? Describe specific geographical areas here.

5. What are subject's tastes in music, books, painting, sports, cars, foods, beverages, films, plants, furniture, houses, politicians, magazines, appliances? What things is subject passionate about?

6. Describe the place or places where subject grew up and spent most of his or her time. (Be particular about this; use small areas such as city blocks or apartment buildings, or neighborhoods, or the geography of a farm. Use only that area with which subject was thoroughly familiar.)

7. Describe subject's attitudes toward the places that have had the most effect on his or her life. Use concrete details here as much as possible.

8. Describe subject's father (as in #1 above). Provide at least three visual scenes of subject's father.

9. Describe subject's mother (as in #1 above). Provide at least three visual scenes here, too.

10. What details of sense perception does subject associate with his or her parents? What physical objects (such as a scarf, a knife, a tree, an ironing board, a bottle) would subject associate with his or her parents?

11. Provide conversations between subject and each of his or her parents.

12. Under what circumstances now does subject think about his or her parents?

13. Describe one or more dreams that subject has had of each of his or her parents.

14. What are subject's attitudes toward his or her parents? How have these changed during subject's life?

15. Describe other members of subject's family who have had a profound influence on subject's life during the first 18 years or so.

16. Provide visual scenes, details of the senses, physical objects, etc., for these other members of subject's family.

17. What is subject's earliest recollection? Be as detailed as possible.

18. What are other early recollections?

19. Describe what subject remembers of his or her childhood prior to beginning school. Try to include at least three events which were of particular importance to his or her life. (Remember to be especially concrete here; render scenes as vividly as possible.)

20. Describe at least three events that were of particular importance to subject's life during his or her elementary

education. Include as much general description of his or her life at that time as is appropriate.

21. Describe at least three events during high school education.

22. Describe subject's passing from childhood into adulthood. Include events which were of particular importance.

23. Describe at least three events which caused subject to be profoundly happy during the first 18 years of his or her life.

24. Three events which caused subject to be profoundly unhappy.

25. What was the absolute best thing that happened to subject in the first 18 years of his or her life? Describe.

26. The absolute worst thing?

27. What are subject's major fears now? Give examples of how these fears have presented themselves to subject and attempt to track them back into subject's childhood as far as possible.

28. What are subject's major pleasures now. Attempt to track these back, too..

29. Describe subject's recurrent or memorable dreams.

30. Describe the circumstances in which subject feels most ill at ease, discontent, unhappy.

31. Describe the circumstances in which subject feels most at ease, content, happy.

32. Describe foolish or silly things subject has done in his or her life.

33. Describe things subject has done in his or her adult life which have required the most profound seriousness.

34. What are subject's attitudes toward money?

35. The opposite sex?

36. Love?

37. Insanity?

38. Suicide?

39. Violence?

40. Family life?

41. Food?

42. Animals?

43. What habits or physical characteristics of other people does subject find most irritating or displeasing?

44. Most attractive or pleasing?

45. What aspects of subject's own character and personality is he or she most at odds with? How do these affect his or her life?

46. What are the motivating forces in subject's life? What are the things that cause subject to do what he or she does?

47. What are subject's ambitions? What are the things he or she is actually striving to attain or to accomplish?

48. What are the major obstacles to subject's ambitions? How do these affect his or her life?

49. What are subject's fantasies? What would subject be if he or she could change his or her life instantly? What kind of life would subject live if he or she could have anything he or she wanted?

50. Describe four or five of the jobs subject has held,

including people with whom he or she worked. Use language peculiar to the jobs. Describe subject's attitudes toward the jobs and the people associated with them.

51. Describe the one person (other than a parent) of the opposite sex about whom subject has cared most.

52. The one person (other than a parent) of the same sex as subject about whom subject has cared most.

53. Describe subject's behavior and thinking when alone, with no possibility of any kind of companionship.

54. When among close friends in a comfortable situation.

55. At a formal party among many strangers.

56. In a strange city.

57. At a wedding.

58. A funeral.

59. At Christmas.

60. In the immediate presence of death.

61. With one other person with whom subject is intimate.

62. In games.

63. In terrifying situations.

64. In awkward situations.

65. When affectionate.

66. When angry.

67. When afraid.

68. When confronted with hostility.

69. When confronted with insanity.

70. When offered affection.

71. In the presence of children.

72. Describe situations, circumstances, behavior, and thinking when subject has had mystical or near-mystical experiences. What are subject's attitudes toward these experiences?

73. Describe subject's major difficulties in dealing with other people, giving specific examples and attempting to track down reasons for these difficulties.

74. What burdens does subject carry, and how does he or she feel about them?

75. Design an ideal landscape for subject.

76. Design an ideal building for subject.

77. Design an ideal human situation for subject.

3 STORY-TRUTH

"**h**ow much of that story is true?" is what I'm likely to be asked after I've given a public reading. It's a naive question, one that irks most fiction-writers. A friend of mine sometimes fires back from the podium, "None of your business!"

But the autobiographical question interests me. My own response to it recently has been, "Eighty-four percent," "Seventy-nine percent," or something like that. I'm not fooling around; I mean to be estimating as exactly as I can the literal truth of the story. What's peculiar is that the interrogation stops there; my percentage answers almost always satisfy both the questioner and the rest of the audience. I never get the inevitable follow-up, "Which parts are true and which aren't?" I can't explain such audience behavior; it seems to me that if someone is bold enough to ask the first question, surely that person or somebody else ought to have the nerve to ask the second.

I'd be ready to try to answer that one, too, as sincerely as I could, because that question interests me most of all. Thirty years of reading serious fiction and twenty years of trying to write it haven't cured me of my own naive curiosity about what's true and what isn't in a good story. When I read "A Good Man Is Hard To Find," I wonder if Flannery O'Connor ever read a newspaper account of a criminal like the Misfit who killed off a whole family. When I read "Goodbye, My Brother," I wonder if John Cheever

ever swatted his brother in the head with something like a piece of seawater-soaked driftwood. When I read "For Esmé, With Love And Squalor," I wonder if J. D. Salinger ever had an intense conversation over tea with an English schoolgirl and her little brother. Not only do I wonder about these possibilities, I also enjoy speculating about them. I'd be willing to bet a fair amount of money that Raymond Carver once had a wild conversation about love with some people who were drinking and sitting around a kitchen table. Part of my reading pleasure comes from guessing about the actual experience upon which the author might have based the parts of his or her story.

So I'm ready to try to answer a reader—or listener—who might be similarly wondering about something in a story of mine. Perhaps perversely, in the eyes of my brother and sister fiction-writers, I feel honored by my audience's curiosity. But in most cases, providing an answer would be a tough assignment for me. When I start writing a story, it's usually based on something I lived through, but as I'm writing it, I quickly forget what actually happened. That kind of truth is useful to me only as a starting point in my thinking about a story. Even though I begin with personal experience, I'm tinkering with it from the first words I set down. When I finish writing—finish the last of the ten to twenty-five or thirty drafts that it takes for me to feel that I've done all I can for my story—my memory of the truth of what happened has been clouded by my many alterations of it.

But not only would I be willing to try to pick out the facts of my fiction, I'd also be interested in what the project might yield. I've written a story based on my getting hit by a car when I was around seven years old; in it I tried to render with some precision my character's experience at the moment of automobile interfacing with child. My forty-year old memory of the original experience is fraught with sensations having to do with weather, landscape, sky, as well as car, gravel, road surface, and human body. *Wanting to move but not being able to make my feet step in any direction, I stand on the side of the road, aware of raising my hands as if to ward off a pillow*... I think I could be persuaded to sit down with the text, examine the sentences and phrases, and try to determine which ones are true to my memory of the experience and which ones are true only to the story I've written.

Then the car brushes me, I spin and fall and see the car sail over the fence into Mr. John Watts's alfalfa field. Picking the truth from such a sentence would take longer than it might seem. My reader and I would have to work out some ground rules for what we understood each other to mean by *memory, truth,* and *imagination.* We'd want to discuss the word *brush* at some length because probably I chose it for its sound and for the image of movement that it conveys, but *brush* also seems to me true to the sensation of *very slight impact* as I remember it. We'd have to talk about *alfalfa* and whether that choice comes out of my original memory, something someone told me later, or an adult liking for the sound of the word and the look of the stuff in a field. All this would be before we even took up the likelihood of a child who has just been knocked down by a car being able to see it sail over a fence.

I'd be up for such a tedious project because I think I'd probably learn something from it. I think my benefit would be similar to what a tennis player gains from watching a slow-motion video of his or her strokes. I wish I had had a chance to sit down with O'Connor, Cheever, or Salinger to examine a passage of one of their stories and to discuss what was remembered and what was imagined in terms of their sentences' diction and syntax; I'm certain I'd have learned a great deal about the "mix" of memory, imagination, language, and epistemology in the individual writer's composition process. I'm pretty sure I'd have felt I was approaching the beating pulse of that writer's art.

But no one has ever read me a sentence of my own work and

asked me to comment on it the way they do in Congressional hearings: "Exactly what is the truth of what you've written here, Mr. Huddle?" When I say, "Forty-three percent," some audience-members nod and grin and get I-thought-so and I-suspected-the-worst-and-now-I-know-I'm-right looks on their faces, but apparently a precise account of what happened and what didn't is not what they want.

My fiction-writing colleagues who resent being asked about the truth of their stories suspect that their achievement is being insulted. I can see their point: if the author admits that the story is mostly true, then the questioner feels that there really wasn't much to the writing, the author simply recorded some history he or she happened to stumble into. If the author says the story is entirely imagined, then the questioner feels there's really not much to that piece of writing, the writer just made it all up: heads, you lose; tails, I win.

I'm usually not insulted, but I am disappointed over my audiences' lack of genuine curiosity about story-truth. "Thinly-veiled autobiography" is a phrase commonly used to bludgeon autobiographical fiction-writers into second-class narrative citizenship, but I think a phrase-by-phrase examination of an autobiographical story's prose would reveal that the discipline of using language to construct experience is even more rigorous when the writer's material is memory than when it is imagination. If carving stone is more difficult than molding clay, then chipping something that really happened into a usable shape for a short story must be at least as much of an accomplishment as making something up.

There is a level at which I'm impatient with these distinctions anyway. At some writers' conference in the future, I'll be the guy who stands up and makes a shaky-voiced speech about how autobiographical writers use immense amounts of imagination and make-it-up-from-scratch writers use memory in every paragraph, and so what are we arguing about anyway, aren't we all in the business of trying to make a good story out of whatever materials we can find? What I want to think is that the bias against memory-writers and in favor of imagination-writers is held almost entirely by critics and book reviewers, and that fiction-writers and ordinary readers understand perfectly well that what matters is the quality of the story, not which brain cell produced it. If I weren't so aggravated over the anti-memory bias, I'd shut up and sit down.

Several years ago, with two writer friends, I drove from Essex Center, Vermont, to Swannanoa, North Carolina. South of Albany, our conversation began to take the form of "life stories." By the time we reached Scranton, we'd formalized the method: one person talked; the other two asked questions. We were well-acquainted with each other's work and generally familiar with each other's lives, so that the conversation penetrated to the heart of crucial issues for each of us, in our lives and (therefore) in our work. When I took a long turn at being the teller, I found myself struggling to explain the small-group politics of my family when my brothers and I were growing up, the ways my relationships with my parents inform my relationships with my children, the elements of my childhood that enabled me to become a writer, and so on. I heard myself making observations that startled me—how had I known and when had I decided these things? The slight pressure of being asked those friendly questions about my life made me search so hard for answers that the occasion was one of personal discovery for me.

But when they took their turns at talking, I was also surprised at the depth of knowledge I gained about my friends, whom I thought I already knew very well. As I listened to them tell their stories, I gained more appreciation of their work; before my mind's eye their books grew in substance, complexity, and subtlety. More than anything else, I came to understand how they had transformed their personal experiences through their writing. I saw what consummate artists they were. In the years since that journey, though I don't see them much anymore, their books have been powerful presences in my life. When I read a new work by one of them, the pleasure I take in it is esthetic, of course, but it is also intensely personal.

Readers don't usually have the option of taking long car-rides with authors; nevertheless, even the sharpest reader's understanding of a story can be enhanced by a useful biographical fact: that Flannery O'Connor was Catholic; that Hemingway was wounded in war; that Raymond Carver and John Cheever had drinking trouble; that Jayne Anne Phillips's brother served in Vietnam; that Andre Dubus served as a Marine officer; that Eudora Welty has lived most of her life in Jackson, Mississippi; that Toni Cade Bambara grew up in New York City; that John Updike worked for *The New Yorker;* that James Alan McPherson and John Casey have degrees from Harvard Law School; that John Gardner rode motorcycles and played the French horn; that John Irving is serious about wrestling and cooking; that Harold Brodkey was an adopted child; and that Stephen King was a high school English teacher—these are facts that enhance the intelligence and the pleasure with which we read these authors' books.

But our hunger for living authors' "life-stories," beyond their practical value, is not much acknowledged in this age of immense critical sophistication. Only recently have I gotten up the nerve to confess that I read fiction mostly for the company of the author. Characters, as far as I'm concerned, never take on lives that are wholly separate from the author; an author is most deeply revealed through his or her most compelling and fully-developed characters. When Flaubert says, *"Madame Bovary, c'est moi,"* he means what he says. Furthermore, I think that personal dimension is the main force that moves most of us to read fiction: intimate human company is what we want when we curl up with a novel or a book of stories. When we say, "I'm reading Flaubert," we mean what we say. The more highly developed our sensibility, the more highly refined our taste in narrative will be, but at a primary level one of us reads Harold Brodkey for the same reason another reads Stephen King. We wish to spend time in the company of the grown-up adopted child or the former high school English teacher.

In choosing to work "close to the bone"—to make narrative out of personal experience—the autobiographical fiction-writer risks working "person-to-person," risks exposing the most essential aspects of himself or herself. Irony is possible, but trickery isn't. Personally vulnerable to the scrutiny of anyone who picks up the book, the autobiographical fiction-writer offers a reader company that is, for better or for worse, sincere and intimate.

Rereading *Where I'm Calling From* recently has deepened my already-high respect for Raymond Carver and his fiction. About halfway through the collection this second time, I suddenly understood that Carver is holding nothing back, is willing to expose all that he is. In this regard, the story that really gets me is a late one, "Intimacy," in which a writer gets down on his knees beside his ex-wife and holds the hem of her dress in his fingers, saying nothing, merely kneeling there on the floor. It's as if with this scene Carver is requesting cosmic forgiveness—and earning it through the deep humility of his art—for all the painful behavior documented in the stories preceding "Intimacy." Even a single reading of his *Selected Stories* will give a reader a profound sense of the struggle Carver waged with alcohol and the victory he won through his essential decency. The struggle, the victory, the decency are not elements that are aside and apart from the experience of reading Carver; they are at the center of his literary achievement. This is something we come to know at almost a subverbal level in reading Carver's short stories.

In spite of what we know instinctively about reading fiction, writers and critics alike speak of literary art as if the relationship between reader and author has no bearing on the act of reading. A friend of mine is willing to tell me personally that her stories are somewhat autobiographical, but she says that if asked about it publicly, she would deny it.

I don't blame her. Story-writers have to protect themselves from readers who are only idly or pruriently curious about the truth of their work. Who would be surprised that the author of a best-selling literary novel that contains some brilliant and bold writing about sex must take an unlisted phone number because of the abusive calls she receives? Sometimes a book provokes readers to feel so much intimacy with the author that they conclude they're entitled to impose on the author (which impulse may explain why J.D. Salinger has chosen to live in seclusion and keep his writing to himself). I can see why my friend thinks the autobiographical truth of her stories is not the business of strangers.

I'm arguing that ultimately the autobiographical truth of a story *is* the business of a reader, and I'm saying that I'm willing to go into the matter of what's true and not true about my own stories. But I'm not about to do it with some stranger who shows up on my front porch and wants to come into my living room to take up the project. And I'm not eager to write a detailed response to somebody I've never met who wants me to discuss the autobiography of a passage in one of my stories.

On the one hand, "How much of that story is true?" is a profoundly anti-art question; it isn't surprising that an artist might be hostile to it. On the other hand, it's a doggedly human question; the fiction-writer who attempts to answer it sincerely is likely to have the rare and perhaps illuminating experience of discussing his or her art in the most basic—most purely human—terms.

Most serious fiction-writers don't think much about their readers when they're actually writing, but they do think about how much of themselves they're giving to their art. Mere technique won't produce stories a writer wants to live with. An esthetic axiom (as applicable to high literature as it is to country music) is that the more of yourself you're able to give your art, the stronger your art will be. So most writers try to locate and use subject matter that brings forth their most passionate feelings, most rigorous thought, most lyric sentences, and most complex vision.

The autobiographical fiction-writer chooses as subject matter material from his or her own life because that material brings forth his or her best writing. This is an instinctive, a necessary choice, because finally what the serious fiction-writer—of whatever inclination—aims to do is to make art that embodies his or her best self. That writer wants a reader to be caught up in what happens in the story, to be engaged by the characters, to be pleased by the sound of the language and by its imagery, to be stimulated by the story's thematic concerns, and to be satisfied by the story's form. These are the means by which that writer hopes to deliver over this "best self" to the reader. This best self embodies everything the writer knows and feels about human aspiration; it is the dearest truth the writer has been able to purchase with his or her esthetic resources.

Foolishly or not, I believe that revealing the exact nature of the material I've used for my stories will not harm me, my family, or my friends, and will not provoke my enemies to take me to court. Why am I so willing to talk? Because to anyone who's seriously curious, I think I can demonstrate something I deeply believe, that autobiographical fiction is the highest form of narrative art. So how much of my story is true? That's a terrific question, sir. Let's sit down right over here and have a look at a paragraph or two. I hope you've got plenty of time.

4 ISSUES OF CHARACTER:
The Saint at the Typewriter

Character has always been the element of fiction that interested me most. The other elements—language, structure, plot—seem to me clearly to belong to Art. Character is the company of other human beings, the experience of living.

I love gossip. I like to talk and hear and think about people. I like to have information about them. I like to see people, see their faces, their bodies, their gestures, their moves. I like to be told or to be able to guess what people are thinking and feeling. I am interested in the scandalous and the foolish, the brutal and fiendish, the brave and intelligent things people do. Of course I take pleasure in the sharing of sensory experience, the meal or the walk taken with a friend. And I am hungry to hear *talk* that seems to me especially true or serious or revealing or just plain pretty to listen to.

My desire to know other human beings and to have access to their experience isn't satisfied with my daily experience, and so I turn to fiction. A variety and an intimacy of experience are available to me in novels and stories. I must speculate about what even my dearest friends and closest relatives are thinking and feeling, but I am able to *know* what Anna Karenina and Emma Bovary think and feel.

Such knowledge as fiction gives me about its characters

satisfies a yearning I have. I've never had much scientific curiosity. I've had a decent enough education, but I've forgotten almost
every important fact I was ever taught. The kind of thing I've
always wanted to know and to remember is the kind of thing that
J. D. Salinger's Sergeant X experiences when he goes inside an
English church to witness a children's choir at rehearsal:

> A dozen or so adults were among the pews, several of
> them bearing pairs of small-size rubbers, soles up, in
> their laps. I passed along and sat down in the front row.
> On the rostrum, seated in three compact rows of audito-
> rium chairs, were about twenty children, mostly girls,
> ranging in age from about seven to thirteen. At the
> moment, their choir coach, an enormous woman in
> tweeds, was advising them to open their mouths wider
> when they sang. Had anyone, she asked, ever heard of a
> little dickeybird that dared to sing his charming song
> without first opening his little beak wide, wide, wide?
> Apparently nobody ever had. She was given a steady,
> opaque look. She went on to say that she wanted *all* her
> children to absorb the *meaning* of the words they sang,
> not just *mouth* them like silly-billy parrots. She then
> blew a note on her pitch pipe, and the children, like so
> many underage weight-lifters, raised their hymnbooks.
> They sang without instrumental accompaniment—or,
> more accurately in their case, without any interference.
> Their voices were melodious and unsentimental, almost
> to the point where a somewhat more denominational
> man than myself might, without straining, have experi-
> enced levitation. A couple of the very youngest children
> dragged the tempo a trifle, but in a way that only the
> composer's mother could have found fault with. I had
> never heard the hymn, but I kept hoping it was one with
> a dozen or more verses. Listening, I scanned all the

children's faces but watched one in particular, that of
the child nearest me, on the end seat in the first row.
She was about thirteen, with straight ash-blond hair of
ear-lobe length, an exquisite forehead, and blasé eyes
that, I thought, might very possibly have counted the
house. Her voice was distinctly separate from the other
children's voices, and not just because she was seated
nearest me. It had the best upper register, the sweetest-
sounding, the surest, and it automatically led the way.
The young lady, however, seemed slightly bored with
her own singing ability, or perhaps just with the time
and place; twice, between verses, I saw her yawn. It was
a lady-like yawn, a closed-mouth yawn, but you
couldn't miss it; her nostril wings gave her away.

Such knowledge as this passage offers a reader seems to me
both deeply satisfying and wildly unpragmatic. It is only in
writerly terms that I can speak of it practically. (The only difference between the fiction-writer and the town gossip, who are
equally interested in this generally unnoticed area of human
behavior, is that the writer *makes* something—namely, novels and
stories—out of his interest.)

So down to practice: here are six ways to bring a character to
life in a story:

1. Information: For example, here we know that Esmé, the
character in this passage from Salinger's story, "For Esmé—with
Love and Squalor," sings in a church choir, is "about thirteen,"
has the best voice of the singers, and is apparently bored.

2. Physical Appearance: Esmé's "ash-blond hair of ear-lobe
length, [her] exquisite forehead, and blasé eyes" are obviously
exemplary details of this category of character-making. That her
"nostril wings" give away her "lady-like... closed-mouth yawn[s]"
is a less obvious and craftier example of character-making: the
detail is minutely precise, it tells a great deal about the personality

of the yawner, and it keeps a reader "seeing" the character. Beginning fiction writers will often provide plenty of description of a character's looks in the paragraph in which they introduce that character. But then, having paid their dues to "details of appearance," they will forget all about what the character looks like for the rest of the story. Salinger is particularly good at using a character's physical presence throughout the whole story so that a reader has a sense of "seeing" the character for the whole story.

3. Thoughts and Feelings: Because of this story's point of view, we don't have direct access to Esmé's mind and heart, but we are given powerful suggestions about what Esmé might be thinking and feeling—by way of her yawning between verses and her "blasé eyes that... might very possibly have counted the house," of our having heard the choir coach speak to her "little dickeybird[s]" and "silly-billy parrots," and our having seen the children raise their hymnbooks "like so many underage weightlifters." So by some very strongly crafted implication we know what Esmé thinks and feels; we don't know it precisely—because she hasn't been able to tell us—but we know it more than generally. Through this whole middle section of the story in which Esmé appears, we know what Esmé thinks and feels, and we are given to know it by way of implication. I consider Esmé one of the dozen or so most vividly portrayed and memorable characters I have encountered in literature. Esmé has taught me a lot about character-making, and here's something new she's taught me on just this most recent reading of the story: when a character is fully realized, a reader knows—because the writer makes the reader know—what that character thinks and feels in whatever situations that character appears; if a reader doesn't know, then the character isn't "all there." This seems to me a principle that must be akin to actors' having to know what their characters are thinking and feeling on stage even when they are keeping quiet and standing off to the side.

4. Actions: In this scene, in which Salinger introduces Esmé into the story, there is no real need to have her *do* anything beyond singing; the only necessity here is for Sergeant X to *see* Esmé, perhaps to pick out her singing voice as being "distinctly separate." But Salinger chooses two small actions for Esmé that make her immediately remarkable: her eyes count the house, and she yawns between verses. These are not actions of high dramatic potency, nor are they especially comical or odd. These are actions that come out of the very center of Esmé's personality. I believe there's a lesson in that, too: characters have only to be themselves to be of interest to a reader; the trick is for the writer to know them so intimately that he can present them "as themselves." To hold a reader's attention a writer doesn't have to make his characters act strange or crazy.

5. Sensory experience: Again, because of the story's point of view, we don't really know what Esmé is smelling, hearing, touching, tasting, and seeing in this passage, though we could probably make some fairly accurate guesses. We know more precisely what she is experiencing intellectually and emotionally than what she is experiencing through her senses. Only occasionally is Salinger a writer for whom Sensory Experience is especially important. I wish he were more exemplary in this department, but since he isn't, the lesson I see here is that if some of a writer's powers of characterization are finely developed, he can get by without having all of them. Salinger is pretty good at five out of the six.

6. Speech: Speech is the characterizing power Salinger most relies upon. Esmé doesn't say anything in the passage I've been discussing, but in the next section she has plenty to say, beginning with "I thought Americans despised tea."

> I'm going to be a professional singer.... I'm going to sing jazz on the radio and make heaps of money. Then, when I'm thirty, I shall retire and live on a ranch in Ohio.... Do you know Ohio?...You're the eleventh

American I've met.... You seem quite intelligent for an American.... Most of the Americans I've seen act like animals. They're forever punching one another about, and insulting everyone, and—You know what one of them did?...One of them threw an empty whiskey bottle through my aunt's window. Fortunately, the window was open. But does that sound very intelligent to you?... My hair is soaking wet,... I look a fright.... I have quite wavy hair when it's dry.... Not actually curly but quite wavy.... Are you married?... Are you very deeply in love with your wife? Or am I being too personal?... Usually, I'm not terribly gregarious.... I purely came over because I thought you looked extremely lonely. You have an extremely sensitive face.... I'm training myself to be more compassionate. My aunt says I'm a terribly cold person.... I live with my aunt. She's an extremely kind person. Since the death of my mother, she's done everything within her power to make Charles and me feel adjusted.... Mother was an extremely intelligent person. Quite sensuous, in many ways.... Do you find me terribly cold?... My first name is Esmé. I don't think I shall tell you my full name, for the moment. I have a title and you may just be impressed by titles. Americans are, you know.... His name is Charles,...He's extremely brilliant for his age.... Sometimes he's brilliant and sometimes he's not,... Charles, do sit up!... He misses our father very much. He was s-l-a-i-n in North Africa.... Father adored him.... He looks very much like my mother—Charles, I mean. I look exactly like my father.... My mother was quite a passionate woman. She was an extrovert. Father was an introvert. They were quite well mated, though, in a superficial way. To be quite candid, Father really needed more of an intellectual companion than Mother was. He was an extremely gifted genius.... Charles misses him exceedingly,... He was an exceedingly lovable man. He was extremely handsome, too. Not that one's appearance matters greatly, but he was. He had terribly penetrating eyes, for a man who was intransically kind.... I'd be extremely flattered if you'd write a story exclusively for me sometime. I'm an avid reader.... It doesn't have to be terribly prolific! Just so that it isn't childish and silly.... I prefer stories about squalor.... I'm extremely interested in squalor.... *Il faut que je parte aussi,*... Do you know French?... I'm quite communicative for my age.... I'm dreadfully sorry about my hair,... I've probably been hideous to look at.... Would you like me to write to you?... I write extremely articulate letters for a person my—... I shall write to you first...so that you don't feel *com*promised in any way.... You're quite sure you won't forget to write that story for me. It doesn't have to be e*xclus*ively for me. It can—... Make it extremely squalid and moving.... Are you at all acquainted with squalor?... Isn't it a pity we didn't meet under less extenuating circumstances... Goodbye,... I hope you return from the war with all your faculties intact.

This monologue I've constructed to illustrate the power of Speech as a characterizing agent. Esmé says all these things in the course of an eleven-page scene. Salinger's writing has many charms, but for the moment I want to focus only on this business of Speech. What Esmé says shows, at the most immediate and engaging level, her intellectual, social, and linguistic precocity. At first glance, this writing might appear satirical, Salinger mocking the English, especially the upper class English, and mocking the young, especially thirteen year old girls. But for all the funniness of these lines of Esmé's and of the scene from which they are drawn, there isn't any mocking, and we readers can feel that in the tone, which is poignant, almost elegiac. What Esmé says, at its deepest level, comes out of grief, out of her reckoning with the loss of her parents: what she says has an outside of cheerfulness, snobbery, pluck, charm, naivete and an inside of sadness, courage, and that quality she's training herself to acquire more of, compassion. More than anything else, Esmé's speech here shows her to be, as she herself might put it, "extremely interesting." She's complicated. What she says shows her to be worthy of our attention and consideration. Fiction-writers who are strong on character first of all have to believe that individual human beings are "extremely interesting," and second of all have to discover and show what it is about them that is interesting. That people have exterior and interior lives which may be poignantly connected is one of the things Salinger's Esmé shows us.

Salinger has been accused of loving his characters more than God would love them, and I expect that's a fair charge. I expect that's one reason why his writing has such a powerful effect on so many of his readers, why his followers are so intense in their devotion to his work. And I expect it's one reason why Salinger's fiction became weaker in his later books and why he's apparently found it difficult to continue his work: love, of that magnitude, must be downright impossible to sustain. "For Esmé—With Love and Squalor" was a kind of turning point in my life. I read it first in 1963 and was right powerfully disrupted by it. I cared about that story so much that I felt in some way as if I possessed it, as if it were mine. I suppose I should be grateful that I wasn't so moved by it that I tried to assassinate a President or something like that. I still have an inordinate affection for the story. I feel that the power it has on me is directly connected to the power of love the author must have invested in it. Love your characters, I could counsel would-be fiction writers, but I know they'd know that was smarmy advice. Either you do or you don't. It's akin to being told by the store manager where you work as a window dresser, "You know, these mannequins will bring in more customers if you invest them with love when you dress them up"; or being told by the head embalmer you work for at the funeral home, "Love your cadavers, your funerals will be more successful." Anyone who would tell you what to do with your love merits your suspicion. Nevertheless, a useful fiction-writing principle can be extracted: if in doubt, treat your characters as if you loved them. If you've got to make some sort of adjustments with your character, try being generous, try letting that character—even if it's a treacherous, nasty-hearted character—be his or her best self, or maybe even *better* than his or her best self.

Speech is something most of us have an interest in and a talent for, if we could just unleash it properly. In a story it can hit a reader just right, can make characters come perfectly into focus like the right twist of a camera lens. Here's a couple in a Raymond Carver story called "Vitamins," a couple we've had some information about but one we really haven't seen clearly together by this point, which is about a quarter of the way into the story:

> Pattie said, "Vitamins." She picked up her glass and swirled the ice. "For shit's sake! I mean, when I was a girl this is the last thing I ever saw myself doing. Jesus, I never thought I'd grow up to sell vitamins. Door-to-door vitamins. This beats everything. This blows my mind."
>
> "I never thought so either, honey," I said.
>
> "That's right," she said. "You said it in a nutshell."
>
> "Honey."
>
> "Don't honey me," she said. "This is hard, brother. This life is not easy, any way you cut it."

That this talk sounds like real talk is one of its virtues. That it articulates the personalities of both characters and of their relationship with each other is another: after reading these lines, we're certain which one is the dominant personality, which one listens to the other and which one doesn't; we could predict with some accuracy what sort of problems this couple is likely to encounter. (Think about it a moment: when you are curious about the relationship between two people, what can tell you the most about it? If you're a romantic and you believe in "flashing eyes" and that sort of thing, you might say, "How they look at each other." But if you're a classicist, and you really want to know the answer to the question, you'll say, "How they talk with each other.") One final virtue of this "Ray Carver talk" is how the flatness of it, the triteness of it, works as a kind of pressure holding in the characters' emotion; the language contains the emotion, limits it in a way that's both sad and explosive.

Another writer who loves a good conversation and who can get the way people talk just exactly right is Eudora Welty. Here's this from "Why I Live at the P.O.":

> "Don't you notice anything different about Uncle Rondo?" asks Stella-Rondo.
>
> "Why, no, except he's got on some terrible-looking flesh-colored contraption I wouldn't be found dead in, is all I can see," I says.
>
> "Never mind, you won't be found dead in it, because it happens to be part of my trousseau, and Mr. Whitaker took several dozen photographs of me in it," says Stella-Rondo. "What on earth could Uncle Rondo *mean* by wearing part of my trousseau out in the road in open daylight without saying so much as 'Kiss my foot,' *knowing* I only got home this morning after my separation and hung my negligee up on the bathroom door, just as nervous as I could be?"

The quality of the talk in Eudora Welty's stories is both ordinary and extraordinary. What her people say seems like what somebody like that would say in that situation, and yet it also seems unusually musical, thingy (which is to say, full of the objects of the world), chirpy, and sociable. The talk in her stories affects me like money on the sidewalk: I want to pick it up and save it and jingle it in my pocket. Here's this from "Lily Daw and the Three Ladies":

> "Lily," said Mrs. Watts..., "we'll give you lots of gorgeous things if you'll only go to Ellisville instead of getting married."
>
> "What will you give me?" asked Lily.
>
> "I'll give you a pair of hemstitched pillowcases," said Mrs. Carson.
>
> "I'll give you a big caramel cake," said Mrs. Watts.
>
> "I'll give you a souvenir from Jackson—a little toy bank," said Aimee Slocum. "Now will you go?"
>
> "No," said Lily.
>
> "I'll give you a pretty little Bible with your name on it in real gold," said Mrs. Carson.
>
> "What if I was to give you a pink crêpe de Chine brassiére with adjustable shoulder straps?" asked Mrs. Watts grimly.
>
> "Oh, Etta."
>
> "Well, she needs it," said Mrs. Watts....

When we speak casually about this kind of talk, we say that Eudora Welty writes "good dialogue." Reviewers will often remark a fiction-writer's "ear" for dialogue, as if all that's involved is to be able to listen carefully to people talking and to transcribe that talk onto the page. That Welty goes well beyond simply writing "good dialogue" or simply having a "good ear" ought to be evident in the *ordering* of the offerings to Lily to keep her from getting married and in how the offerings appeal to various of the human appetites: "a pair of hemstitched pillow-cases... a big caramel cake... a souvenir from Jackson—a little toy bank... a pretty little Bible with your name on it in real gold..." And then consider the presentation of the ultimate temptation: "'What if I was to give you a pink crepe de Chine brassiere with adjustable shoulder straps?' asked Mrs. Watts grimly." The *grimly* here is priceless. The *grimly*—the adverb that goes with a *said* or an *asked*, the little unit of grammar that bad writers love to use badly and that good writers learn not to use at all—here is evidence of this writer's being, as Esmé would put it, "an extremely gifted genius." Eudora Welty's great gift, the thing that sets her apart from her distinguished peers, Carson McCullers, Flannery O'Connor, and Katherine Anne Porter, is her range and agility with language. And one of her major contributions to story writing is that she has expanded the limits of what characters may say in a story; she is bold enough to allow her characters to speak as characters in stories have not heretofore spoken:

> "Listen!" whispers Powerhouse, looking into the ketchup bottle and slowly spreading his performer's hands over the damp, wrinkling cloth with red squares. "Listen how it is. My wife gets missing me. Gypsy. She goes to the window. She looks out and sees you know what. Street. Sign saying Hotel. People walking. Somebody looks up. Old man. She looks down, out the window. Well?... *Ssssst! Plooey!* What she do? Jump out and bust her brains all over the world."
>
> He opens his eyes.
>
> "That's it," agrees Valentine. "You gets a telegram."
>
> "Sure she misses you," Little Brother adds.
>
> "No, it's nighttime." How softly he tells them! "Sure, it's the nighttime. She say, What do I hear? Footsteps walking up the hall? That him? Footsteps go on off. It's not me. I'm in Alligator, Mississippi, she's crazy.

Shaking all over. Listens till her ears and all grow out like old music-box horns but still she can't hear a thing. She says, All right! I'll jump out the window then. Got on her nightgown. I know that nightgown, and her thinking there. Says, Ho hum, all right, and jumps out the window. Is she mad at me! Is she crazy! She don't leave *nothing* behind her!"

"Ya! Ha!"

"Brains and insides everywhere, Lord, Lord."

All the watching Negroes stir in their delight, and to their higher delight he says affectionately, "Listen! Rats in here."

"That must be the way, boss."

"Only, naw, Powerhouse, that ain't true. That sound too *bad*."

"Does? I even know who finds her," cries Powerhouse. "That no-good pussyfooted crooning creeper, that creeper that follow around after me, coming up like weeds behind me, following around after me everything I do and messing around on the trail I leave. Bets my numbers, sings my songs, gets close to my agent like a Betsy-bug; when I going out he just coming in. I got him now! I got my eye on him."

"Know who he is?"

"Why, it's that old Uranus Knockwood!"

"Ya Ha!"

"Yeah, and he coming now, he going to find Gypsy. There he is, coming around that corner, and Gypsy kadoodling down, oh-oh, watch out! *Ssssst! Plooey!* See, there she is in her little old nightgown, and her insides and brains all scattered round."

A sigh fills the room.

"Hush about her brains. Hush about her insides."

"Ya! Ha! You talking about her brains and insides—old Uranus Knockwood," says Powerhouse, "look down and say Jesus! He say, Look here what I'm walking round in!"

They all burst into halloos of laughter. Powerhouse's face looks like a big hot iron stove.

"Why, he picks her up and carries her off!" he says.

"Ya! Ha!"

"Carries her *back* around the corner..."

"Oh, Powerhouse!"

"You know him."

"Uranus knockwood!"

"Yeahhh!"

"He take our wives when we gone!"

"He come in when we goes out!"

"Uh-huh!"

"He go out when we comes in!"

"Yeahhh!"

"He standing behind the door!"

"Old Uranus Knockwood."

"You know him."

"Middle-size man."

"Wears a hat."

"That's him."

Everyone in the room moans with pleasure...

Powerhouse has exotic powers of speech that enable him to say everything from "Boogers" to the words of the despairing tale of his wife, Gypsy, who "jumps out the window" and "bust[s] her brains all over the world." Powerhouse, in the joyful noise he makes out of his powerful gloom, is at the center of this music, this scene, this story, but the others in that bar in "Alligator, Mississippi," on that rainy night, are given charming, intricate riffs of language; they all contribute to the sound of that fantastic conversation. The experimental aspect of "Powerhouse" is the way the limits of language have been extended so as to make words—and in particular, human speech—evoke music, jazz music, blues, improvisation in which various people contribute various elements of the whole musical sound. But this is experiment in the service of the entirely traditional element of the story, character; the story "presents" Powerhouse, demonstrates his extraordinariness.

What we casually call "dialogue," what I am trying to elevate in significance by calling it "Speech" here, is the quintessential human act. As Faulkner says in his Nobel Prize acceptance speech,

> ...when the last ding-dong of doom has clanged and faded from the last worthless rock hanging tideless in the last red and dying evening,...even then there were will be one more sound: that of [man's] puny inexhaustible voice, still talking.

And John Cheever, in the admirable ending of his not-especially admired novel, *Falconer*, accomplishes the final steps of his main character's figurative resurrection through the "drunken palaver" of a stranger. Farragut manages to escape from Falconer prison by substituting himself for a dead man and zipping himself into a burial sack. Outside, unzipping himself from the death of his prison existence, Farragut makes his way back to life with this encounter:

> The stranger was utterly inconsequential, beginning with his lanky hair, his piecemeal face, his spare, piecemeal frame and his highly fermented breath. "Hi," he said. "What you see here is a man who is being evicted. This ain't everything I own in the world. I'm making my third trip. I'm moving in with my sister until I find another place. You can't find nothing this

late at night. I ain't been evicted because of non-payment of rent. Money I got. Money's the one thing I don't have to worry about. I got plenty of money. I been evicted because I'm a human being, that's why. I make noises like a human being. I close doors, I cough sometimes in the night, I have friends in now and then, sometimes I sing, sometimes I whistle, sometimes I do yoga, and because I'm human and make a little noise, a little human noise going up and down the stairs, I'm being evicted. I'm a disturber of the peace."

"That's terrible," said Farragut.

"You hit the nail on the head, "said the stranger," you hit the nail on the head. My landlady is one of those smelly old widows—they're widows even when they got a husband drinking beer in the kitchen—one of those smelly old widows who can't stand life in any form, fashion, or flavor. I'm being evicted because I'm alive and healthy. This ain't all I own, by a long shot. I took my TV over on the first trip. I got a beauty. It's four years old, color, but when I had a little snow and asked the repairman to come in, he told me never, never turn this set in for a new one. They don't make them like this any more, he said. He got rid of the snow and all he charged me was two dollars. He said it was a pleasure to work on a set like mine. It's over to my sister's now. Christ, I hate my sister and she hates my guts, but I'll spend the night there and find a beautiful place in the morning. They have some beautiful places on the south side, places with views of the river. You wouldn't want to share a place with me, would you, if I found something beautiful?"

That Cheever locates redemption in the speech of this nutty, drunken stranger is of course ironic, but it seems to me a special, fiction-writer's kind of irony. To accomplish the work of fiction-writing, the writer must become the ultimate democrat, the ultimate Christian: the fiction-writer can't condemn anybody. A state of suspended moral sensibility is necessary to take on the business of character-making. The fiction-writer's motto must be, as Stanley Elkin puts it, "Everybody has his reasons." In our regular, walking-around, gum-chewing lives, we're used to proceeding with all of humanity divided into *them* and *us*. *They* are everybody we don't know, don't understand, don't like, don't approve of; *they* aren't kin to us; *they* have less money than we do or more money than we do; *they* do and think and say and feel things differently. However, when we sit down to write fiction, everybody has to become us. We must imagine the lives of people who are *other* than ourselves, and to do so we must become them, they must become us.

This transformation that must come about in a fiction-writer's moral attitude is not one that is consciously elected. It begins, as many of the larger issues of fiction-writing begin, with a technical problem, in this case the problem of getting the details right: the cold-blooded murderer whose story we mean to tell will not become real for us as writers or as readers unless we can see many of the details of his life with precision; once we begin to imagine the details, we begin to see things his way, we begin to understand his reasons. The more we make this character come alive in our story—the more we fill in the details of information about him, his physical appearance, his thoughts and feelings, his actions, his sensory experience, and his speech, the more we *become* this character. The transformation is a given dynamic of fiction-writing. But I do not mean to say that anybody who attempts to write fiction will undergo such a transformation. If a writer does not give himself or herself over to the material and to the characters, then the transformation will not come about and the fiction will fail. If the writer keeps that distance between himself or herself and the murderer, the murderer will not become a living, convincing character, and the story won't work.

So the fiction-writer must be open to experience other than his or her own. As a result of such opening up, the writer will usually manage to avoid certain mistaken attitudes that result in shallow characterization or obviously manipulative plotting. The transformed fiction-writer won't try to condemn a character or a type of character. The transformed writer won't condescend, or write down, to his characters. The transformed writer will avoid simplifying his characters in order to make some abstract point, will ignore the boring limitations of stereotype. The transformed fiction-writer will be more likely to choose characters who are at least his or her equal. The transformed writer carries his characters' burdens, takes responsibility for their actions, forgives them their trespasses, and fights for their rights. This miracle of the transformed writer occurs, I assert, because in the conscientious making of characters and their fictional world, the saint at the typewriter tries to get the details right.

5 LET'S SAY YOU WROTE BADLY THIS MORNING

...don't feel bad, Ramos
What's done is did
That's all right, son
Ya git another chance tomorrer. —Michael Casey
"The Company Physical Combat
Proficiency Test Average"
Obscenities

In September 1986, I had a novel rejected. In October of the same year, I had that rejection on my mind as I watched the American and National League baseball playoffs. A new television set allowed me to see what I had never really noticed before, the facial expressions of the players. What particularly intrigued me was how batters look when they strike out and how pitchers look when they give up a home run.

In that incredible American League fifth game, just after the Red Sox substitute center fielder Dave Henderson, with two strikes and two balls on him, had hit that ninth inning homer, the camera switched to a close-up of Angels relief pitcher Donnie Moore. I have never seen such visible anguish. Moore is a veteran, a man who gives the appearance of being quiet, proud, and possessed of a great deal of hard-earned skill. There was in his face at that moment the sign of a crushed spirit. I wondered how Donnie Moore could ever make himself pitch to another batter.

Getting my novel rejected was not at all similar to what I imagine was Donnie Moore's experience of pitching a ninth-inning, game-winning home-run ball to Dave Henderson. My publisher, David Godine, gave me the bad news in straightforward fashion as he and I drove home from a day's fishing on the Lamoille River in Vermont. Godine had sat on the manuscript for eight months, time enough for me to imagine many and various scenarios of his discussing the book with me. The rosiest of these fantasies had him writing me a check on the spot for a six-figure advance; the bleakest had me committing suicide right in front of him upon hearing that he didn't want to publish the book.

In actual fact, the news was much worse than I expected—not only did Godine not want to publish the novel himself, he also thought it would be a dreadful mistake for me to let anyone publish the novel—but my feelings were not even vaguely suicidal. I think I'd known for a long while that my novel was weak. Consciously I'd hoped that an editor might be able to give me suggestions so that I could revise it to make it a good novel. Unconsciously I think I wanted somebody to tell me to put the thing away. In this regard Godine obliged my deepest desires. Earlier in the day he'd also caught more fish than I had.

I figure I worked on the novel for an average of about three hours a day for 10 months—let's say I had about 900 hours of writing time invested in that 307-page manuscript. That's not counting the time I spent thinking about it while I walked around or lapsed into a reverie over it while driving to the grocery store or solved some difficult problem in it with my subconscious mind while I slept.

As novels go, mine was written pretty efficiently. Ten years is not an outrageous amount of time for a writer to work on a book— Hannah Green, my old teacher at Columbia gave that much of her life (say, conservatively, about 11,000 writing hours) to *The Dead of the House,* and Ralph Ellison apparently has been working on his second novel for more than twenty years. But Ann Beattie is said to have done one of her novels in about a month, and one can imagine Isaac Asimov starting a book on Monday and mailing the finished manuscript to his publisher the following Monday.

In my adult life I've written something in the neighborhood of forty or fifty short stories, of which I've published maybe twenty-five. There are only a few stories I still have on hand—ones that haven't found a home—that I can remember with any clarity. Usually when they aren't much good, I recognize that after they've gathered a couple of rejections, and I either revise them or put them away.

But this is the first novel I've ever written, and my immediate plan for it is to put it away. My theory about these matters is that if there's anything worthwhile in that manuscript, it will stick in my mind enough to send me back to the novel in a year or two. If there isn't anything worthwhile there, then I'll forget all about it and let the manuscript gather dust.

In consigning this manuscript to a desk drawer, I am comforted by the behavior of baseball players. There are *no* pitchers who do not give up home runs, there are *no* batters who do not strike out. There are *no* major league pitchers or batters who have not somehow learned to survive giving up home runs and striking out. That much is obvious.

What seems to me less obvious is how these "failures" must be digested, or put to use, in the overall experience of the player. A jogger once explained to me that the nerves of the ankle are so sensitive and complex that each time a runner sets his foot down, hundreds of messages are conveyed to the runner's brain about the nature of the terrain and the requirements for weight distribution, balance, and muscle-strength. I'm certain that that ninth-inning home run that Dave Henderson hit off Donnie Moore registered complexly and permanently in Moore's mind and body. The next time Moore faced Henderson or faced a similar circumstance, his pitching was informed by his awful experience of October 1986. Moore's continuing baseball career depended to some extent on his converting that encounter with Henderson into something useful for his pitching. I can also imagine such an experience destroying an athlete, registering in his mind and body in such a negative way as to produce a debilitating fear.

There are a few examples of writers who for one reason or another were stopped in their work. The Fugitive poet and critic John Crowe Ransom stopped writing original verse in his mid-thirties, though he tinkered with his old poems, making little changes here and there, for the rest of his life. After the publication of *Gone With the Wind,* Margaret Mitchell devoted her writing energy to answering her fan mail. A few years ago a young man named John Kennedy Toole drove to Milledgeville, Georgia, to commit suicide after his novel had been turned down a number of times; that book, *A Confederacy of Dunces,* was posthumously published to considerable acclaim. And will somebody please tell me what has happened to Harper Lee, author of nothing since her wonderful *To Kill a Mockingbird*?

However sturdy the human body may be, it is also immensely delicate. Any little malfunction—say, for example, one ever-so-slightly damaged nerve in an ankle—can cause the apparatus to break down significantly: the unhittable 95 m.p.h. fastball can become the immensely hittable 83 m.p.h. not-so-fastball. For an athlete to perform well, he must be able to extend himself out into a territory in which he is immensely vulnerable.

One of the many ways in which athletes and artists are similar is that, unlike accountants or plumbers or insurance salesmen, they must perform at an extraordinary level of excellence if they are to achieve even a small success. They must also be willing to extend themselves irrationally in order to achieve that level of performance. A writer doesn't have to write all-out all the time, but he or she must be ready to write all-out any time the story requires it. Hold back and you produce what just about any literate citizen can produce, a "pretty good" piece of work. Like the cautious pitcher, the timid writer can spend a lifetime in the minor leagues.

And what more than failure—the strike out, the crucial home run given up, the manuscript criticized and rejected—is more likely to produce caution or timidity? An instinctive response to painful experience is to avoid the behavior that produced the pain. To function at the level of excellence required for survival, writers like athletes must go against instinct, must absorb their failures and become stronger, must endlessly repeat the behavior that produced the pain.

It's not merely a matter of putting the failed work behind you and going on; what you must do is convert the energy of a failed past work into usable energy for present and future work. Consider the hypothetical case of Donnie Moore having to pitch to Dave Henderson again in a crucial situation: instead of simply putting the 1986 experience behind him, Moore, according to my theory, could convert his memory of the 1986 home run into pitching brilliantly to Henderson. Not only would Moore have "learned from his experience," he would also have been charged with the energy of it.

Easy to say: put failure to use. How does one do it? One notion I can offer has to do with what I'll call "esthetic luck"—a sibling of "athletic luck."

Esthetic luck is random and two-headed. No writer, no matter how accomplished, can be certain when sitting down to work that the results of extreme effort will be writing of high quality. One can school oneself in the literature of one's tradition, train oneself to a high level of technical skill, construct ideal working circumstances of time and place, regularly come to the writing desk rested, alert and in good health, achieve a state of brutal self-honesty, open one's mind to every possibility of concept and language, and nevertheless write one lousy line after another. Conversely (and perversely) one may pick up a napkin in a bar to make a few notes and suddenly find oneself writing fabulous stuff. The odds of writing well are a great deal better if the writer is well-prepared, but there's never a guarantee of good writing.

If production is the first of the two heads of esthetic luck, then the second is reception: Even if one has the good fortune to complete a fine piece of writing, there's a good chance it will go unrecognized by anyone else. Fine poems and stories and novels are rejected all the time. The story goes that *Catcher in the Rye* was turned down by twenty publishing houses before it found a taker. A much-admired poet acquaintance of mine says that while the best journals accept some of her work, they usually reject what she knows to be the best poems in any sheaf she submits to them. My opinion is that fine work can always find someone to recognize its value, but some looking is usually required. A strong manuscript may have to be sent to fifty editors before it reaches the one who recognizes its value. But it takes a pretty tough-skinned writer to send a work out again after the forty-ninth rejection.

There's a story that someone once asked the poet Richard Wilbur how he dealt with rejection slips and he confessed that he didn't know because he'd never received one. This seems to me such a necessary anecdote that if it didn't already exist we'd have to invent it. If esthetic luck is truly random—meaning that no matter what we do we can't assure ourselves we'll write well and that even if we write well we can't count on anyone's recognizing our achievement—it stands to reason that somebody somewhere would have to harvest nothing but good fortune.

What I think is valuable about understanding the crazy nature of esthetic luck is that it can be just as encouraging as it is discouraging. Understanding esthetic luck is the key to serenity for a writer. Let's say you wrote badly this morning, and the mail brought you a rejection slip for a sheaf of poems and an insulting note paper-clipped to a returned short story and another note from an editorial assistant at a publishing house explaining that somehow the manuscript of your novel has been misplaced, they're sorry they've taken a year to let you know this, but that the editor you sent it to in the first place has been fired, and so there's no need, really, to send them another copy. Lots of sensible people would take such a morning as a clear sign that there are better ways to spend one's time than in trying to write well. But our ideally serene writer will read the same evidence to make the opposite case: if your luck is bad today the odds are improved that you'll get good luck tomorrow.

Esthetic luck is the major argument in favor of working through a process of revising a piece of writing through many drafts. If you're a supremely talented artist and you hit a very lucky day, then maybe you can write a poem or story or chapter of a novel that needs no revision. If you're a regular writer with your appointed portion of esthetic luck, you'll need to come at the piece again and again. I like to think of revision as a form of self-forgiveness: you can allow yourself mistakes and shortcomings in your writing because you know you're coming back later to improve it. Revision is the way you cope with the bad luck that made your writing less than excellent this morning. Revision is the hope you hold out for yourself to make something beautiful tomorrow though you didn't quite manage it today. Revision is democracy's literary method, the tool that allows an ordinary person to aspire to extraordinary achievement.

Revision of course is not an option for athletes. In my opinion, baseball players would be able to offer more testimony to the capriciousness of athletic luck than the players of any other game. My most outrageous notion on this matter is that the crazy luck of baseball accounts for the significance of its players' spitting: to spit is to change one's chemistry, to cast out the immediate past, to set oneself to face the future. In their thinking, batters and pitchers must proceed in a logical manner: they consider the scouting reports and the opinions of their coaches and fellow players; they consider "the last time up," along with the history they have shared in all their previous encounters; they make adjustments; they spit for luck.

In the overall balance of esthetic luck, by my calculations, the bad outweighs the good by a ratio of about 17 to 1, but the good nevertheless exists. Somebody who worked hard for years with little visible success suddenly gets a contract and publishes a fine book that is well-reviewed and that almost makes it to *The New York Times* bestseller list; this somebody wins prizes and fellowships, receives invitations to lecture. For every version of this happy story, there are seventeen hard-working literary citizens who have given a considerable portion of their lives to the practice of their art, every one of them with artistic gifts in various stages of development. All seventeen have had the experience of writing well on a regular basis; not one of them has had much success at publishing.

Something at issue here is a peculiarly American misconception about talent, that either you have it or you don't—if you have it, performance is an effortless matter for you, and if you don't have it, you're hopeless. One of the most destructive archetypes of the American consciousness is "The Natural," the person who can do something perfectly without even trying; a sibling of "The Natural" is "The Discovery," a person who finds out he or she has this perfect ability or who is discovered by an expert to have it. From experience, I can tell you that the most common motivating factor for people attending the Bread Loaf Writers' Conference is to find out whether or not they "have what it takes."

What the great American game of baseball seems to me to demonstrate most obviously is that those who "have what it takes" must nevertheless work hard at their craft all the time and that many who might have been judged not to "have what it takes," through hard work at their craft, can also perform well. Recent years of World Series and league championship games have shown us great hitters and pitchers hitting and pitching badly while players we've never heard of perform beautifully. What veteran baseball players and writers know is that constantly working hard will produce a respectable batting or earned run average, a stack of pages of substantial literary value, an acceptance from a good journal.

I am not describing a method of achieving happiness. I am describing a necessary and healthy way for a few people to carry out their lives; happiness has nothing to do with it. What seems to me the only legitimate goal of any would-be writer is to achieve a circumstance of ongoing work, the serenity to carry out the daily writing and revising of what poems, stories, or novels are given you to write. On those occasions when your serenity seems about to collapse, I recommend that you step out into your back yard and vigorously spit.

FIRST EPILOGUE:

In September, 1987, I returned to my novel manuscript to attempt a revision. About halfway through reviewing the manuscript, I realized that it was indeed a novel I didn't want to work on any more and didn't want ever to publish. I put it away permanently.

SECOND EPILOGUE:

After "Let's Say You Wrote Badly This Morning" appeared in the January 31, 1988, issue of *The New York Times Book Review,* I found the letters of response I received to be uncommonly moving and illuminating. Relevant excerpts from these letters are as follows:

> I wonder if you know Branch Rickey's famous comment: "Luck is the residue of design."
> I have always felt that the greatest baseball players (i.e. Willie Mays) are those who are able to give themselves

over most fully to the game in the present moment. It may be called "instinct," or it may be called artistic absorption (i.e. Willie Mays in centerfield or at the plate or on the base paths).

—David Moats
Rutland, Vermont

Let me offer you a quote by Phil Niekro. During Niekro's first season with the Yankees, a *Times* reporter asked him the key to baseball longevity. Niekro mentioned, of course, his knuckleball, but he also said that his attitude played a major role in providing himself with such a long career. "I try to accept my losses without being defeated," Niekro said.

—Jim Tackach
Bristol, Rhode Island

I think I will go outside and spit
Until I get the hang of it;
Then I will write far into the night
Until I get the damned thing right
And if I do not get the hang of it
I'll just go outside and take another spit!

—Sarge Sterling
Philadelphia, Pennsylvania

As a baseball fan and the author of a novel that has recently been rejected by nearly as many houses as 'Catcher in the Rye,' and as the son of a novelist who has been working on his third novel for the past 28 years, let me say…. [a]fter all is said and done, I think spitting in the backyard might be the ultimate solution.

—Thomas Sancton
New York, New York

Your terms "esthetic luck" and "athletic luck" should be expanded to include "scientific luck." My mentor, Fritz Lipmann (Nobelist, 1953), asked me a penetrating question before accepting me as a graduate student in his laboratories at Rockefeller University—"How Lucky are you?" My answer is obvious by the fact that I spent a decade with Lipmann.

At a recent memorial symposium for Fritz in Berlin the issue of "luck" surfaced again and again. Werner Maas of NYU medical center recalled an outing with Freda and Fritz Lipmann in the Adirondacks the weekend in October before Lipmann received the call from Stockholm. Fritz disappeared into a field of clover as Werner and Freda impatiently hiked on. He caught up with them thirty minutes later with a four leaf clover in hand and talked excitedly about how lucky he always was in the lab and the field!

—Peter Pennett
Gainesville, Florida

I went into my 9 a.m. freshman comp class and had all my students vigorously spit. It was messy, but it did change the chemistry of the class.

—Cathryn Amdahl
Pullman, Washington

And also baseball bears witness to the small *victories* that go unmarked, in life or in writing. The way Henderson danced around the bases—that's the way I feel when words work, when a line in a poem seems just right. Whether or not I will have the "esthetic luck" to share the words with a larger audience, the elation of that particular moment goes unmarked and unshared—unlike baseball, where we can all witness Henderson's glee.

—Wendy Mnookin
Chestnut Hill, Massachusetts

...so far as I'm concerned the only similiarity between writers and athletes is that they both scratch their privates in public.

—Fred Bruning
Long Island, New York

Your article appeared two days after I received a most damning review of what I felt to be an excellent research proposal (I am a chemist). I have been silently slinking through the hallway between my office and lab, fearful that a colleague may stop me and ask what my score was.

...I must not, as I was tempted to do, ignore the damning review letter. I must continue to write proposals, and they must be clearly and well written. The critique I received must fuel the fires of my efforts. And each morning, before I begin, I shall go out to the loading dock of our lab facility for a good spit.

—Clare Biswas
Beltsville, Maryland

I remember the look on Moore's face, too. Somebody just knocked off my new manuscript of poems this very morning. I just stepped outside the office and harked up a mighty gob. You are right! It works. Onward!

—Paul Zimmer
Iowa City, Iowa

I erred, though, following your advice a couple of evenings later. It was -25 , the drifts were high, my aim

was off, and the spittle damn near broke my toe!
—Lee Richardson-Ross
Concord, Vermont

On Thursday of this week I received a rejection slip from *The Atlantic* for the first short story I have ever sent out. It has taken me four years to feel I was ready to send one and it took them three months to decide they didn't like it....

I now think I will purchase a bucket for every room in my house, labeled SPIT.
—Judy Darke Delogu
Portland, Maine

I am a cardiologist. I [have] take[n] care of desperately ill, fragile patients all my working life. I have patients die every week, and sometimes several; and this is quite typical for cardiologists. And let me agree with you, "...what seems to me less obvious is how these 'failures' must be digested..." I don't know how I go on, or how anyone "takes the hit," as we say in medicine; how someone can literally walk away from a cooling body in one room and be as 100% ready to give one's best when one walks into the next room. Something complex registers on the mind and body of Donnie Moore when his pitch is swatted into the bleachers; and something complex gets registered on our minds when we attend the post-mortem examinations of those of our cases which end unfavorably. Yet we go on; and I am quite a cheerful and vigorous physician.

If a ballplayer consistently hit .400, he'd be in Cooperstown. If I hit .400, I'd be in prison.
—Name Withheld

Warren [Spahn] told me the following story: the once-Boston Braves wound up spring training one year by playing a game, in Boston, against the Red Sox. Spahn faced Ted Williams once and struck him out with a letter high fast ball over the outside corner. Afterward, Williams and Spahn chatted and Ted remarked, as they parted, "By the way, that fast ball you got me on was a great pitch."

Several years later, Spahn faced Williams again, this time in a clutch situation with men on base, late in the All Star game. Warren told me he did not consciously remember Williams' earlier comments, but Warren's subconscious knew just which pitch to throw, and he threw it. As Williams trotted around the bases after he belted the game winning home run, he was grinning at Spahn; puzzled at first, the light bulb lit up, and Warren yelled, "You Son-of-a-Bitch, you set me up!" Williams laughingly acknowledged it.

—Harvey J. Blumenthal
Tulsa, Oklahoma

THIRD EPILOGUE:

From page B-12 of *The New York Times* of July 20, 1989: "A Ball Player's Life Turns on a Home Run," by Michael Levy:

It was one pitch in one game during the course of a successful 13-year professional baseball career. But some of Donnie Moore's friends and teammates say that ever since he threw that pitch, giving up a home run that cost the California Angels an important playoff game in 1986, Moore had been on a downward spiral.

According to those interviewed, the spiral was forged by a complicated mixture of marital problems, financial strains, and the inevitable decline in athletic ability that comes with age. Moore was 35 years old and had been released by a minor league baseball team when, on Tuesday afternoon, he argued with his wife in the kitchen of their suburban Anaheim home, pulled a pistol, shot her three times and then killed himself.

"I think insanity set in," said Dave Pinter, Moore's longtime agent. "He could not live with himself after Henderson hit the home run. He kept blaming himself."

6 THE FINELY SHADED PROSE OF KATHERINE MANSFIELD'S
"The Garden Party"

Style is the means by which a story makes its reader perceive and feel many things all at once. Even more than what happens in it, the way in which a narrative is recounted determines its effect on a reader. In a rich, complex story like Katherine Mansfield's "The Garden Party," style is such a subtle power that seeing how it works requires carefully monitoring almost every sentence of it.

From the opening "And after all the weather was ideal," giddy anticipation is the mood of "The Garden Party." The Sheridan family's preparation for the party requires approximately eleven and a half pages of description, whereas the party itself begins and ends in half a page. The story's opening sets forth the weather, the sky, the season. In the middle of the first paragraph, an image is delivered in one deft sentence, the writerly equivalent of one of those Corot paintings so small and so finely detailed that a viewer must stand no more than a foot or two away to see it properly:

> The gardener had been up since dawn, mowing the
> lawns and sweeping them, until the grass and the dark flat
> rosettes where the daisy plants had been seemed to shine.

A reader sees this gardener, and the results of his labor, from a distance, as if looking down on him from an upstairs window. One of Mansfield's primary resources is her visual artistry; not only does she make the world of her story intensely visible, she does it with maximum efficiency. Speed is important to this story, and so in one sentence she paints what another writer might accomplish in three or four.

The gardener at work in the distance is the right image for the reader to hold in mind while entering the story. One of its major thematic concerns is class differences, the tension between workers and masters. Throughout the "preparation" phase of the story, masters scurry about, concerning themselves with frivolous matters, while workers carry out the labor necessary for their masters' ritual of pleasure. Mansfield explicates the tension with the lightest of hands and with a delicate irony. The servant-master relationship here, in turn-of-the century New Zealand, is an old-fashioned colonial one, almost as ideal for the masters as the day's weather.

From the initial "And after all," we readers are in the company of the Sheridans, seeing things from their point of view, experiencing the story through the chatty language of Sheridan sensibility: "As for the roses, you could not help feeling they understood that roses are the only flowers that impress people at garden parties..." This sensibility is so privileged that its standards for being impressed by flowers are very high, and "you" are being addressed as if "you" shared the same values. The "tilt" of the language (the sensibility) is sufficient to affect us readers, to amuse and charm us with the Sheridans' innocence, and to invite us to imagine how the workers might view the Sheridans. But finally we attend this garden party as the Sheridans' guests, and we can't help humoring them, even collaborating with them by seeing just exactly what they mean, understanding exactly how they feel. The language won't allow us any other role; we're insiders whether we like it or not.

For instance, if the story's one-sentence second paragraph read, "The men arrived, ready to put up the marquee, while the

Sheridans were still eating breakfast," we would have an entirely different perception of the circumstance than the one we actually receive from the sentence of the text: "Breakfast was not yet over before the men came to put up the marquee." In the former case, we would be standing impatiently outside with the men, irked at the decadence of people who'd still be dawdling over breakfast at this hour. In the latter case, we're at the table with the Sheridans, rushing to swallow our last bites and irked at having to deal with workmen at such an inconvenient hour. Mansfield's sentence gives the impression of being an objective report, but its point-of-view shading is her trick. With hundreds of other more and less shaded sentences, she maneuvers readers into kinship with the Sheridans.

For its reader, as well as for its protagonist, Laura, the story is an education in Sheridanism, the primary source of which is the mother. Though a minor character, the mother is crucial in her role of defining what it means to be a Sheridan. When asked where she wants the marquee put, Mrs. Sheridan replies,

> "My dear child, it's no use asking me. I'm determined to leave everything to you children this year. Forget I am your mother. Treat me as an honored guest."

This four-sentence speech establishes both a character and a set of values. Mrs. S. is affectionately ironic toward her children. She aspires to be irresponsible and pampered. She's nervy and witty enough to present herself this way, as insufferably spoiled and wanting to be even more so. She's cunningly providing her children with on-the-job training in the giving of garden parties. As readers, we may be mildly horrified by this *grande dame*, but we're also amused by her. We withhold judgment of her because she has let her guard down. The gardener may toil in the distance, but Mrs. S. sits right beside us at the breakfast table, treating us to an intimate view of her personality.

If we've cooperated with Mrs. Sheridan in her desire to be treated as an "honored guest," we can hardly refuse the private, familial logic that prevents two of the sisters from telling the men where to put up the marquee:

> But Meg could not possibly go and supervise the men. She had washed her hair before breakfast, and she sat drinking her coffee in a green turban, with a dark wet curl stamped on each cheek. Jose [whose name, incidentally, is probably pronounced as if it were spelled "Josie"], the butterfly, always came down in a silk petticoat and a kimono jacket.

At this point in the story, we've been drawn into a deep absurdity: the issue here is merely to decide where to put this thing and to convey that decision to the men who will do the work of putting it up. Mrs. Sheridan could have said, "Tell them to put it there by the karakas," and a daughter could have shouted her order back through the kitchen. But, as the story goes on instructing us, the Sheridans are who they are—people of a certain class—and such simple matters of decision-making and communicating take on the consequence of enormous labor.

The image that embodies that absurdity is the "piece of bread-and-butter" Laura ("the artistic one") carries with her when, having been dispatched by her mother and sisters, she goes out to deal with the workmen. Mansfield establishes Laura as the story's protagonist with the sentence "It's so delicious to have an excuse for eating out of doors, and besides she loved having to arrange things; she always felt she could do it so much better than anyone else." With one exception, Laura Sheridan is the only character in the story to whose inner life we readers have access. Ultimately it is Laura's story, and this "so delicious" sentence is the moment of her taking possession of it. Henceforth we experience the story in the close company of Laura. We never know exactly how old she is, but we see her as being somewhere in the vicinity of fourteen to sixteen. Already we know enough about her mother and her sisters not to be surprised that Laura feels she can arrange things "so much better than anyone else."

Four workmen await Laura's direction, sketched in sufficient detail for us to understand how Laura might be taken aback by them: "They carried staves covered with rolls of canvas, and they had big tool-bags slung on their backs." Although the main source of tension in the story is class-difference, a subtle secondary source is gender-difference. Both sources inform this tableau—of a young girl facing four grown workmen, the girl at least in theory, by virtue of her class, holding authority over the men:

> Laura wished now that she had not got the bread-and-butter, but there was nowhere to put it, and she couldn't possibly throw it away. She blushed and tried to look severe and even a little bit short-sighted as she came up to them.

If we've been quickly and efficiently drawn into the social fabric of the world of "The Garden Party," we've also been drawn closer to Laura. We appreciate her youthful exuberance and naivete. ("How very nice workmen were! And what a beautiful morning! She mustn't mention the morning; she must be businesslike.") And we appreciate her bemused monitoring of her place in this world, her ongoing attempts to figure out exactly how things work, or how they ought to work. ("Laura's upbringing made her wonder for a moment whether it was quite respectful of a workman to talk to her of bangs slap in the eye. But she did quite follow him.") We understand that in this encounter with the workmen, Laura is in a little over her head, but she's equipped with wits and poise, she's sensitive to every nuance of their exchange, and she's *learning* immensely from it. She's carrying out an apprenticeship, and we have become involved in the process of her learning. Since we witnessed her mother's witty high-handedness, we are now aware of how Laura is shadowed by her mother in this exchange with the workmen, and we like Laura all the more for her clumsy apologies for her privileged life. ("'Only a very small band,' said Laura gently. Perhaps he wouldn't mind so much if the band was quite small.")

We are also touched by Laura's intense response to the world around her:

> And [the karaka trees] were so lovely, with their broad, gleaming leaves, and their clusters of yellow fruit. They were like trees you imagined growing on a desert island, proud, solitary, lifting their leaves and fruits to the sun in a kind of silent splendour.

The beauty of the natural world stimulates Laura's imagination. Such description makes us see this "garden" in the moment of Laura's seeing it, thereby making us unusually aware of her youthful vitality.

The last sentence of the paragraph describing the karaka trees asks the question, "Must they be hidden by a marquee?" and the beginning of the next paragraph answers the question, "They must. Already the men had shouldered their staves and were making for the place." There's a cheerful wit at work here; obviously this question-and-answer registers Laura's thinking of the moment, but it also seems to come from a more disinterested "witness." We readers are both inside and outside Laura's consciousness in these moments. "The Garden Party" depends on a reader's apprehension of Laura's experience both from within and from without, a simultaneous identification with its protagonist and an objective witnessing and judging of her from some distance.

So by the middle of the third page a reader has been made aware of Laura's family values and her apprenticeship in those values, her youth, sensitivity, imagination, her almost unconscious wit, her status as a representative from the world of women to the world of men, and her exact place in this society of unequal but ironically benign division of power between the classes:

> Only the tall fellow was left. He bent down, pinched a sprig of lavender, put his thumb and forefinger to his nose and snuffed up the smell. When Laura saw that gesture she forgot all about the karakas in her wonder at him caring for things like that—caring for the smell of lavender. How many men that she knew would have done such a thing? Oh, how extraordinarily nice workmen were, she thought. Why couldn't she have workmen for friends rather than the silly boys she danced with and who came to Sunday night supper? She would get on much better with men like these.

The reader's response to Laura has become increasingly complex. Here we see her being condescending, as befits her class, but also romantic and idealistic, as befits her age. We suddenly understand how limited her world is; even though she's privileged enough to attend dances, she's known only a few "boys" of her own class. Of course she makes too much of the workman's "caring for the smell of lavender"; nevertheless, we judge Laura's ignorance not to be of the stupid, dangerous variety but instead to be sweet and admirably humane.

Then we encounter one of Mansfield's overtly stylish sentences: "It's all the fault, she decided, as the tall fellow drew something on the back of an envelope, something that was to be looped up or left to hang, of these absurd class distinctions." With Laura's thought left suspended through that long dependent clause, we are pinned to the moment, watching the tall fellow's artwork right along with Laura. And since we have to wait for it, the phrase "these absurd class distinctions" gains some emphasis. At the same time, the lengthy interruption undercuts Laura's conviction; it conveys the impression that her condemnation of class distinctions is such a casual matter that her mind can stray even while it makes the observation. That undercutting carries over into her observations that follow: "Well, for her part, she didn't feel them. Not a bit, not an atom...." Well, for our part, since we've seen that she has class distinctions very much on her mind, we understand her not to be stating a fact but to be coaching herself toward a more democratic sensibility. Laura is impelled toward both truth and illusion. She's both noble and silly:

> Some one whistled, some one sang out, "Are you right there, matey?" "Matey!" The friendliness of it, the—the—Just to prove how happy she was, just to show the tall fellow how at home she felt, and how she despised stupid conventions, Laura took a big bite of her bread-and-butter as she stared at the little draw-ing. She felt just like a work-girl.

When Laura is called to the phone, Mansfield transports her with a gorgeous sentence, using exactly the right verb for Laura's state of mind as well as for her physical movement and using a syntax that makes a reader see her moving through the elements of her world: "Away she skimmed, over the lawn, up the path, up the steps, across the verandah, and into the porch. In the hall..." she meets her father and brother; the text doesn't tell us she's breathless but these stacked-up prepositional phrases make us register her exertion almost physiologically.

After Laurie admonishes his sister to "Dash off," Laura is instantly transported to the telephone with the two-word para-graph opening, and we are in that bemused circumstance of over-hearing one half of a conversation:

> The telephone. "Yes, yes; oh yes. Kitty? Good morn-ing, dear. Come to lunch? Do, dear. Delighted of course. It will only be a very scratch meal—just the sandwich crusts and broken meringue shells and what's left over. Yes, isn't it a perfect morning? Your

white? Oh, I certainly should. One moment—hold the
line. Mother's calling."

We've seen Laura with her mother, with the workmen, then
with her brother; now we add this conversing-with-her-friend-
over-the-phone facet of her personality to our composite portrait
of her. What's the essence of her conversation? Well, surface
(sandwich crusts), fluff (broken meringue shells), quintessentially
worldly and unessential matters (your white); in short, the stuff of
a party. Probably no teenage girl should be held spiritually to
account for her phone conversations with her pals, and in this
case a reader is almost charmed by the utter vacuousness of
Laura's remarks. Her mother's interruption is entirely in the spirit
of Kitty and Laura's concern with the superficial:

> Mrs. Sheridan's voice floated down the stairs. "Tell
> her to wear that sweet hat she had on last Sunday."
> "Mother says you're to wear that *sweet* hat you had
> on last Sunday. Good. One o'clock. Bye-bye."

Dutiful daughter that she is, Laura repeats her mother's direc-
tive to Kitty, with added emphasis on the word *sweet* comically
underscoring the general theme—at the same time it ascribes to
"that sweet hat" a symbolic value—of worldly superficiality. This
hat of Kitty's is probably a distant cousin of the hats that Laura's
father and brother were brushing in the hallway a few paragraphs
earlier, and it is certainly a sibling of the hat of consequence that
will enter the story half a dozen pages later. Mansfield manages
her hat symbolism with impeccable delicacy and timing, so that
at this point in the story we are receiving our initial instructions
in how to perceive hats. It's important that the symbolism start
working in our minds; it's also important that we don't really
notice how it's working. Mansfield executes an ingeniously gradual pedagogy: the story teaches us to think about hats in such a
way that when, at the end of the story, we're asked a significant

question about a hat, without knowing how it came to us, we suddenly find that we know the answer.

Another of Mansfield's major resources as a writer is her ability to render a character's inner "state" through that character's perception of the world:

> She was still, listening. All the doors in the house
> seemed to be open. The house was alive with soft,
> quick steps and running voices. The green baize door
> that led to the kitchen regions swung open and shut
> with a muffled thud. And now there came a long,
> chuckling absurd sound. It was the heavy piano being
> moved on its stiff castors. But the air! If you stopped to
> notice, was the air always like this? Little faint winds
> were playing chase, in at the tops of the windows, out
> at the doors. And there were two tiny spots of sun, one
> on the inkpot, one on a silver photograph frame, play-
> ing too. Darling little spots. Especially the one on the
> inkpot lid. It was quite warm. A warm little silver star.
> She could have kissed it.

This passage conveys a powerful sense of the house—not so much what it looks like (though it does some of that, too) but what it feels like to be inside it and paying attention to it. More importantly, it conveys Laura's solitude in this rare moment of her very social day, her being alone and in immensely good spirits.

Indeed, this part of the story conspires to build the perfection of Laura's happiness toward ecstasy:

> There, just inside the door, stood a wide, shallow
> tray full of pots of pink lilies. No other kind. Nothing
> but lilies—canna lilies, big pink flowers, wide open,
> radiant, almost frighteningly alive on bright crimson
> stems.
> "O-oh, Sadie!" said Laura, and the sound was like a

little moan. She crouched down as if to warm herself at
that blaze of lilies; she felt they were in her fingers, on
her lips, growing in her breast.

The word *blaze* has been earned here by the previous paragraph's progression through "pink... pink... radiant... [and]
bright crimson". If Laura's response to the lilies has a sexual
dimension, it is also a deliciously innocent, wholehearted
embracing of the world. But with these lilies, the natural world
and the Sheridan world have been perversely united: highhanded
Mrs. Sheridan has authored these flowers: "I was passing the shop
yesterday, and I saw them in the window. And I suddenly thought
for once in my life I shall have enough canna lilies."

A significantly intimate moment in this mother-daughter relationship occurs here so quickly that, in spite of its peculiarity, a
reader barely registers it:

Sadie had gone. The florist's man was still outside at
his van. She put her arm round her mother's neck and
gently, very gently, she bit her mother's ear.
"My darling child, you wouldn't like a logical
mother, would you? Don't do that. Here's the man."

As with the lilies, this gesture of Laura's toward her mother is
both sexual and innocent. The character of their intimacy is possible
only in the paradise of this one morning of Laura Sheridan's life,
when she is poised between childhood and adulthood and when she
is in perfect accord with the world and her mother. We know that
Laura's values ("Perhaps he wouldn't mind so much if the band was
quite small") are at odds with Mrs. Sheridan's ("...for once in my
life I shall have enough canna lilies"), but here we see the mother
and daughter in a moment of unusually affectionate accord—or
rather we see Laura expressing an unusually intimate and playful
affection toward her mother while Mrs. Sheridan tolerates her
daughter's gesture only until the flower man carries in more lilies.

With another efficient "jump-cut," we find ourselves "In the drawing-room [with] Meg, Jose and good little Hans," moving the piano and other furniture. Having seen how ineffectual Laura has been in directing the workmen as to where to put up the marquee, we're now able to observe with what aplomb her sister takes on the role of mistress:

> "Hans, move these tables into the smoking-room, and bring a sweeper to take these marks off the carpet and—one moment, Hans—" Jose loved giving orders to the servants, and they loved obeying her. She always made them feel they were taking part in some drama. "Tell mother and Miss Laura to come here at once."
> "Very good, Miss Jose."

The voice here is that of an (unlimited) omniscient narrator, one who presents it as a fact that the servants "loved obeying" Jose. The scene belongs entirely to Jose, who carries out a little rehearsal "just in case I'm asked to sing this afternoon." The occasion is one of Mansfield's most deftly rendered set-pieces:

> *Pom*! Ta-ta-ta! *Tee*-ta! The piano burst out so passionately that Jose's face changed. She clasped her hands. She looked mournfully and enigmatically at her mother and Laura as they came in.
>
> > *This Life is* Wee-*ary,*
> > *A Tear—a Sigh.*
> > *A Love that* Chan-*ges,*
> > *This Life is* Wee-*ary,*
> > *A Tear—a Sigh.*
> > *A Love that* Chan-*ges,*
> > *And then... Good-bye!*
>
> But at the word "Good-bye," and although the piano sounded more desperate than ever, her face broke into a brilliant, dreadfully unsympathetic smile.

> "Aren't I in good voice, mummy?" she beamed.
> *This Life is* Wee-*ary,*
> *Hope comes to Die.*
> *A Dream—a* Wa-*kening.*

Jose's death-informed song so bizarrely contrasts with the lively mood of the house (and of the story so far) that the effect is comic. This scene is an introduction of the death/mortality *motif* that eventually becomes the story's primary concern, but this introduction (like that of the hat-symbolism) is carried out so light-handedly that a reader hardly notices what is being accomplished. Jose is clearly more interested in the polish of her performance than in the content of her song. And the scene further contrasts Jose with Laura; they are apparently close in age, yet we immediately remark how intense Jose's concern is with appearances, whereas we have seen a fair portion of Laura's attention given to the natural world and to her rich inner life. When Laura takes the sandwich flags into the kitchen, she finds

> …Jose there pacifying the cook, who did not look at all terrifying.
> "I have never seen such exquisite sandwiches," said Jose's rapturous voice. "How many kinds did you say there were, cook? Fifteen?"
> "Fifteen, Miss Jose."
> "Well, cook, I congratulate you."
> Cook swept up crusts with the long sandwich knife, and smiled broadly.

A reader must admire how adroitly Jose flatters cook into a good mood and how precisely and economically Mansfield has drawn this miniature narrative—"How Jose Pacified Cook." Jose's choice of the word *exquisite* is as calculated to manipulate cook as is Mansfield's *rapturous* to convey to the reader exactly the right shade of irony in perceiving Jose's operations. Jose's voice sounds overly enthusiastic to us, but we understand that it is music to cook's ears, as is the inflatedly formal "I congratulate you." Cook's gesture of sweeping "up crusts with a long sandwich knife" is the dramatic demonstration of her embarrassed pride.

Sadie's announcement that "Godber's has come" is followed by several observations that, although they are probably Laura's thoughts, seem to originate from a kind of collective Sheridan consciousness:

> That meant the cream puffs had come. Godber's were famous for their cream puffs. Nobody ever thought of making them at home.

The illusion of the collective Sheridan consciousness then associates itself more particularly with Laura and Jose, linking the girls and giving the impression that these sisters are like-minded, at least when it comes to cream puffs:

> Of course Laura and Jose were far too grown-up to really care about such things. All the same, they couldn't help agreeing that the puffs looked attractive. Very. Cook began arranging them, shaking off the extra icing sugar.

That final detail is designed to make the reader share with Laura and Jose the enticement of these cream puffs. However much they might agree about "such things," the individual personalities of the sisters also come to bear on this consideration of the cream puffs:

> "Don't they carry one back to all one's parties?" said Laura.
>
> "I suppose they do," said practical Jose, who never liked to be carried back. "They look beautifully light and feathery, I must say."
>
> "Have one each, my dears," said cook in her comfortable voice. "Yer ma won't know."

Laura's meditation on eating cream puffs gives the impression of being a process of thought she shares with Jose, so that again we see the sisters in a state of intense accord:

> Oh, impossible. Fancy cream puffs so soon after breakfast. The very idea made one shudder. All the same, two minutes later Jose and Laura were licking their fingers with that absorbed inward look that only comes from whipped cream.

The amusing last phrases of the paragraph have the effect of drawing the reader into the sisters' experience. Under the influence of taking this shared pleasure with Jose, Laura invites her sister to accompany her "to see how the men are getting on with the marquee. They're such awfully nice men." We've seen enough of how differently these sisters relate to the servants to be able to anticipate a lack of accord in their view of the marquee-installers. That anticipated lack of accord, however, must be momentarily put on hold because "Something had happened."

Now Mansfield must construct a tableau that will significantly prepare the Sheridan girls (and the reader) for the news to come:

> "Tuk-tuk-tuk," clucked cook like an agitated hen. Sadie had her hand clapped to her cheek as though she had toothache. Hans's face was screwed up in the effort to understand. Only Godber's man seemed to be enjoying himself; it was his story.

This is a vision of such clarity that a reader can imagine these servants arranged Stage Right in a small group with a spotlight having just come up on them, Laura and Jose moving toward them out of the spotlight Stage Left that illuminated the two of them "licking their fingers with that absorbed inward look."

The story teases us for a few lines, as Laura is teased, before Godber's man delivers the juicy details:

> "What's the matter? What's happened?"
> "There's been a horrible accident," said cook

"A man killed."

"A man killed! Where? How? When?"

But Godber's man wasn't going to have his story snatched from under his very nose.

This delay adds gravity to the news when it finally is delivered. Here the story insists that we note how Godber's man, though of the same class as the killed man, has taken possession of the story of the death and how instead of expressing grief, compassion, or shock, he takes pleasure from the telling of the story:

> "Know those little cottages just below here, Miss?" Know them? Of course, she knew them. "Well there's a young chap living there, name of Scott, a carter. His horse shied at a traction-engine, corner of Hawke Street this morning, and he was thrown out on the back of his head. Killed."
>
> "Dead!" Laura stared at Godber's man.
>
> "Dead when they picked him up," said Godber's man with relish. "They were taking the body home as I come up here." And he said to the cook, "He's left a wife and five little ones."

This is almost the mid-point of the story, and it is a significant turning point. Until now Laura's morning has been devoted to frivolous matters—supervising the installation of the marquee, chatting with Kitty on the phone, appreciating the canna lilies, hearing Jose's rehearsal, and sampling the cream puffs in the kitchen. From here on out, Laura must address herself to the matter of death. There is a delicious and dark irony in Godber's man being the deliverer of both the cream puffs and the news of the death. Godber's man's insensitivity to the news that he brings underscores Laura's extreme response to it:

> "Jose, come here." Laura caught hold of her sister's sleeve and dragged her through the kitchen to the

other side of the green baize door. There she paused
and leaned against it. "Jose!" she said, horrified,
"however are we going to stop everything?"

"Stop everything, Laura!" cried Jose in astonish-
ment. "What do you mean?"

"Stop the garden-party, of course." Why did Jose
pretend?

A further irony is that we have come to know "practical" Jose
well enough to anticipate her response to the idea of stopping the
garden party, but we've also seen how Laura, in sharing the cream
puffs with Jose, has mistakenly come to think of them as seeing
things similarly. Remember, Laura was about to take Jose out to
meet her pals the marquee-installers. One of the ways we come to
apprehend Laura so intensely is through contrasting her with the
people around her—with her mother earlier, with Godber's man
more recently, with her brother later on, and with Jose here:

But Jose was still more amazed. "Stop the garden-
party? My dear Laura, don't be so absurd. Of course
we can't do anything of the kind. Nobody expects us to.
Don't be so extravagant."

Jose's view of the circumstance may be overly practical for
our taste, but she does have a point; Godber's man would be the
first to agree with her that the working people would not expect
the Sheridans "to stop the garden-party." But emotionally we
can't help siding with Laura:

"But we can't possibly have a garden-party with a
man dead just outside the front gate."

This issue of whether or not the Sheridans should hold the
garden party is not easy to resolve; still more difficult is the question of exactly what gesture the Sheridans ought to make toward
the bereaved family.

Extravagant is the word that Jose uses to characterize Laura's notion that the garden party *should be stopped*; it is the same word that Laura uses three lines later, in an interior monologue, to characterize the notion that the garden party *should go on* "with a man dead just outside the front gate." One can imagine Jose's and Laura's having picked the word up (probably from their mother) because of its sonic appeal to their precocious adolescent sensibilities. But the word is peculiarly accurate in both girls' use of it, though their notions are directly opposing. With its now-obscure first level of meaning—"wandering beyond limits or bounds; roving"—*extravagant* becomes a sort of "key word," appearing significantly a number of times throughout the story. *Extravagance* has a special place in the canon of Sheridanism: these are people who for an afternoon's party will have a marquee installed, hire a band, hire extra waiters, order many trays of canna lilies from a florist, serve fifteen different kinds of sandwiches, and order cream puffs from Godber's, and yet, as Jose and Laura indicate to us here, they are wary of being (or appearing) *extravagant*. Mansfield takes special care to place the word at the beginning of a paragraph depicting poverty as seen through the lens of Sheridanism:

> [Having "a garden-party with a man dead just outside the front gate"] really was extravagant, for the little cottages were in a lane to themselves at the very bottom of a steep rise that led up to the house. A broad road ran between. True, they were far too near. They were the greatest possible eyesore, and they had no right to be in that neighborhood at all. They were little mean dwellings painted a chocolate brown. In the garden patches there was nothing but cabbage stalks, sick hens and tomato cans. The very smoke coming out of their chimneys was poverty-stricken. Little rags and shreds of smoke, so unlike the great silvery plumes that uncurled from the Sheridans' chimneys.

Washerwomen lived in the lane and sweeps and a cobbler, and a man whose house-front was studded all
over with minute bird-cages. Children swarmed. When
the Sheridans were little they were forbidden to set foot
there because of the revolting language and of what
they might catch. But since they were grown up, Laura
and Laurie on their prowls sometimes walked through.
It was disgusting and sordid. They came out with a
shudder. But still one must go everywhere; one must
see everything. So through they went.

This passage accomplishes a number of narrative tasks. It
makes a reader see the world outside the Sheridan gates—and
see it through Sheridan eyes. (The comparison of the two classes
of chimney smoke is particularly vivid.) Because it is her meditation, the passage makes us revise our sympathetic impression of
Laura. (Can this be the same girl who has wanted to "have workmen for friends"?) It reminds us that though she may have
momentary democratic impulses, Laura has been raised a
Sheridan; she has her mother's values (and phrasing!) at the center of her consciousness. It prepares a reader for Laura's later
journey into this neighborhood and her return from it in the company of her brother. It even suggests how the Sheridans must be
viewed by the people of that neighborhood by inviting a reader to
envision the sweeps' and cobbler's and washerwomen's children
stopping their swarming play to observe Laura and Laurie touring
the neighborhood with their nostrils twitching.

Still, we do not ascribe it to pure hypocrisy when Laura continues arguing with Jose, "And just think of what the band would
sound like to that poor woman." (The band, apparently, still troubles her from her earlier conversation with the marquee-
installers.) In spite of—or maybe even because of—her sounding
immature and silly when she articulates her non-Sheridan
impulses, we're in sympathy with her; the story has maneuvered

us into an involvement with her struggle against the weight of elitist values by which she has been raised. The struggle may be a puny one—because after all, she is still very young—but we are persuaded that it is genuine, that there is something in Laura that on occasion doesn't love being a Sheridan.

When Jose responds to Laura's last point, we see the unleashing of the author's formidable satirical ability:

> "Oh Laura!" Jose began to be seriously annoyed. "If you're going to stop a band playing every time some one has an accident, you'll lead a very strenuous life. I'm every bit as sorry about it as you. I feel just as sympathetic." Her eyes hardened. She looked at her sister just as she used to when they were little and fighting together. "You won't bring a drunken workman back to life by being sentimental," she said softly.

Here it is Jose's assertion of feeling "every bit as sorry" and "just as sympathetic" but revealing "hardened" eyes that immediately puts her out of the reader's favor. The *sympathetic* followed two words later by *hardened* is where the author has most brutally stacked the deck against her as an individual. Mansfield's having Jose use the word *strenuous* reinforces what we've already remarked of the Sheridans' view of labor; to work is to decide where to put a marquee, to write sandwich flags, or to pacify cook: by such standards, of course, "to stop a band playing" might be seen as strenuous. And while being outrageously unjust, Jose's use of the word *drunken* (probably spoken "softly" so as not to be overheard by the servants) is mitigated considerably by our suspicion that it is not so much individual meanness as a general Sheridan impulse on certain occasions to connect that word with *workman*, and by Jose's having some truth on her side in pointing out that Laura can't bring the man back to life. The preceding sentence suggests that this debate has fallen to the level of a sibling quarrel; we can envision Laura and Jose as little girls having a spat:

"Drunk! Who said he was drunk?" Laura turned furiously on Jose. She said, just as they had used to say on those occasions, "I'm going straight up to tell mother."

"Do, dear," cooed Jose.

Given what we've just seen of Jose's insisting that she's sympathetic while her eyes turn hard, *cooed* is the perfect word for the moment. The very sound of the sentence, with its three long-voweled syllables followed by the short two-syllable snap of Jose's name, is a musical rendering of classical sisterly taunting.

The sentence that immediately follows Jose's taunt is Laura's asking, "Mother, can I come into your room?" What's remarkable here is Mansfield's system of instant transportation. We don't see Laura flounce away from Jose and rush up the steps and down the hallway to her mother's door. Instead, she's instantly there, asking permission to come in.

A sure sense of timing is what allows Mansfield unobtrusively to eliminate conventional transitions. With this same sense of timing, she's able to introduce an apparently insignificant element into the story, leave it unmentioned for several passages so that it passes out of the reader's immediate memory, then bring it back into the story with an almost mysterious resonance attached to it. For instance, Laura's eating bread-and-butter when she was talking with the marquee-installers is associated later with her eating cream puffs with Jose and wanting "to see how the men are getting on with the marquee." For a more significant instance, here, at some almost unnoticeable level of memory, we are recalling Laura's telephone conversation with Kitty ("Mother says you're to wear that *sweet* hat...") when

...Mrs. Sheridan turned round from her dressing table. She was trying on a new hat.

"Mother, a man's been killed," began Laura.

"*Not* in the garden?" interrupted her mother.

"No, no!"

"Oh, what a fright you gave me!" Mrs. Sheridan sighed with relief, and took off the big hat and held it on her knees.

This passage reinforces the ironically paradoxical connection between frippery and death that Mansfield established when she had Godber's man deliver both the cream puffs and the news of the dead carter. The hat serves as a prop for Mrs. Sheridan, further signifying her concern only with the temporal and the worldly; the hat enhances our amusement over Mrs. S.'s momentary fear that the death might have occurred on the actual site of the party. The scene also corrects some of the negative impression we took from Laura's Sheridanesque portrait of the neighborhood outside her family's gate and deepens our sympathy for her. We've begun to understand how alone she is in her concern for the dead workman. As this scene goes on, with Laura "Breathless, half-choking," and telling "the dreadful story," we see her more and more as a child appealing to her mother for parental wisdom. Mrs. Sheridan offers her version of it:

"But, my dear child, use your common sense. It's only by accident we've heard of it. If some one had died there normally—and I can't understand how they keep alive in those poky little holes—we should still be having our party, shouldn't we?"

The "true" Sheridan attitude shines through in Mrs. S.'s little aside, which calls to a reader's mind Laura's phrasing in describing that neighborhood ("the greatest possible eyesore"). Mansfield established a context for a reader's apprehension of the phrase "those poky little holes" with the scene much earlier in the story where Laura sat alone after her phone conversation and happily listened to steps, voices, and shutting doors in this Sheridan house that is vast enough to contain "regions." We can feel how Mrs. Sheridan is defeating Laura in spite of the child's impulse toward decency:

Laura had to say "yes" to that, but she felt it was all wrong. She sat down on her mother's sofa and pinched the cushion frill.

On a literal level this last sentence is unremarkable, but the story has operated on us in such a way that figurative associations are called up by Laura's sitting *on her mother's sofa* and *pinch[ing] the cushion frill*. These shadowy associations convey to us the exact texture of Laura's emotional and intellectual distress. This is the moment when she presents an argument that Mrs. Sheridan cannot logically defeat: "Mother, isn't it really terribly heartless of us?" What follows is inspired strategy on the part of Mrs. S.:

"Darling!" Mrs. Sheridan got up and came over to her, carrying the hat. Before Laura could stop her she had popped it on. "My child!" said her mother, "The hat is yours. It's made for you. It's much too young for me. I have never seen you look such a picture. Look at yourself!" And she held up her hand-mirror.

Mansfield is manipulating the reader with a skill that is even more consummate than Mrs. Sheridan's in manipulating her daughter. From the ear-biting scene, we know how Laura adores her mother. From the bread-and-butter scene, we know how concerned with her appearance Laura is. And from the careful introduction and development of the symbolism, we've begun to understand the significance of the hat. "Don't take the hat!" we long to shout to her, as if it were an offering from a fairy-tale witch. But how can she resist? Her mother offers it out of a love we know Laura craves. It transforms her into the beautiful creature we expect she yearns to be. It is a "charm" to make death invisible.

But she does resist, winning the reader's admiration. She doesn't "look at herself; she turn[s] aside." And recognizing defeat, her mother stops her dissembling manipulation and resorts to mere pouty scolding:

> "You are being very absurd, Laura," she said coldly. "People like that don't expect sacrifices from us. And it's not very sympathetic to spoil everybody's enjoyment as you're doing now."

When Laura says, "I don't understand," and walks out of her mother's room and into her own bedroom, we understand her to have been strong enough to resist her mother's manipulation. We're all set to breathe a sigh of relief and we're prepared to face further suffering on Laura's part. But wait!

> "There quite by chance, the first thing she saw was this charming girl in the mirror, in her black hat trimmed with gold daisies, and a long black velvet ribbon. Never had she imagined she could look like that. Is mother right? she thought.

This part of the paragraph works like a magician's illusion. Because we never saw her take off the hat and because she has been preoccupied with the issue of stopping or holding the party, we share Laura's surprise and momentary metaphysical dislocation upon confronting the "charming girl in the mirror." Earlier, Mansfield refrained from describing the hat, saving these details of the ribbon and the daisies for this moment of presentation. In this powerfully visual story, physical descriptions of the main characters have been almost completely omitted. We've never seen what Laura looks like, and even now we don't see *her*. But the details of the hat convey the power of the vision she confronts in the mirror. Laura's response to what she sees is more innocence than pure narcissism since her initial impression is not of herself but of "this charming girl." Vanity in Laura Sheridan's character is almost involuntary; instead of seeking her own image in the mirror, she sees it "quite by chance." And that chance enables the witch's offering to cast its spell after all. Her thoughts jump from "Never had she imagined she could look like that" to "Is Mother right?" The rightness here takes on a shrewd ambiguity: right about how Laura looks in the hat—but also right about the correct attitude to take toward the workman's death. In this moment we're with Laura alone, not judging her from a distance but intimately receiving her perceptions and following her responses:

> And now she hoped her mother was right. Am I being extravagant? Perhaps it was extravagant. Just for a moment she had another glimpse of that poor woman and those little children, and the body being carried into the house. But it all seemed blurred, unreal, like a picture in a newspaper. I'll remember it again after the party's over, she decided. And somehow that seemed quite the best plan...

Within this paragraph Mansfield has executed one of the more difficult maneuvers of narrative writing. She has explicitly demonstrated a character's change of mind. Laura herself isn't even fully aware of the change, but clearly at the beginning of the paragraph she is opposed to the party, while at the end of the paragraph she has accepted it. We readers are right there in the circuits of her brain, watching the change come about. It is the look of herself in that hat that sways her, and so superficial concerns win out over the solemn business of giving death its due. Vanity (even though involuntary) has the power to make this young girl participate in something she knows to be "really terribly heartless." To her credit, she does a bit of wrestling with that old Sheridan bugaboo "extravagance," during which struggle she experiences some empathy with the dead carter's family. But extravagance isn't really the issue, and the empathy she experiences isn't powerful enough to defeat the hat's influence over her. At the end of the paragraph, we recognize how the better part of Laura—that vulnerable and only partially emerged democratic impulse—has been defeated. The hat has made her a Sheridan again. But because we've so intimately shared her experience of these moments, we don't condemn her at all (as, remember, we condemned Jose for claiming sorrow and sympathy while "hardening" her eyes). On the contrary, Laura's defeat, her fall back into Sheridanism, seems a deeply human failing. Our sympathy toward her is not unlike what we'd feel for a fairy tale princess who falls under a witch's spell. Laura tries, she really does her best, and it is only because she's unfairly ambushed by her mother and her own involuntary vanity that she fails.

Time slows down for Laura's meditation before the mirror. Now that Laura has changed her mind, Mansfield speeds time up again with a transition that is necessary because the elements it connects (Laura meditating and the party beginning) are too disparate to connect "instantly." Even so, the author doesn't dawdle:

> Lunch was over by half past one. By half past two they were all ready for the fray. The green-coated band had arrived and was established in a corner of the tennis-court.
>
> "My dear!" trilled Kitty Maitland, "aren't they too like frogs for words? You ought to have arranged them round the pond with the conductor in the middle on a leaf."

The word *fray* keeps us readers inside the Sheridan circle; as the party approaches, they refer to it jokingly as the opposite of what their efforts are aimed toward making it be. We remember from the earlier telephone conversation that Kitty was coming for lunch, and Laura's superficial way of speaking to her in that conversation has prepared us for Kitty's superciliousness—*trilled* quickly and intensely conveys an impression of Kitty's personality. Kitty even demands that we readers apprehend her connection between the green-coated band-members and her demeaning fantasy of them as frogs.

The flame of Laura's conscience flickers once more before the party begins, when her brother returns home:

> At the sight of him Laura remembered the accident again. She wanted to tell him. If Laurie agreed with the others, then it was bound to be all right. And she followed him into the hall.
>
> "Laurie!"
>
> "Hallo!" He was half-way upstairs, but when he turned round and saw Laura he suddenly puffed out his cheeks and goggled his eyes at her. "My word, Laura; you do look stunning," said Laurie. "What an absolutely topping hat!"
>
> Laura said faintly "Is it?" and smiled up at Laurie, and didn't tell him after all.

This is not, by any means, a turning point; the passage conveys Laura's seeking reassurance over the decision that she reached while standing before the mirror. But again we see the enormous power of the hat over her; if her appearance has been drastically improved by it—as Laurie's response indicates that it has—her democratic impulses have been severely diminished by it. More subtly, the passage reinforces Mansfield's ironic portrait of this subtle sister-brother relationship: Laura looks to Laurie for ethical guidance—she imagines that he is a person of substance—but here we see Laurie as being just as devoted to matters of appearance as Jose and Mrs. Sheridan. This little exchange is of narrative value at the moment, but it is also essential in preparing a reader for the story's final scene.

The eleven and a half pages that have taken us up to this point have been in anticipation of the event heralded by the story's title. Now let us attend the garden party from beginning to end:

Soon after that people began coming in streams. The band struck up; the hired waiters ran from the house to the marquee. Wherever you looked there were couples strolling, bending to the flowers, greeting, moving over the lawn. They were like bright birds that had alighted in the Sheridans' garden for this one afternoon, on their way to—where? Ah, what happiness it is to be with people who all are happy, to press hands, press cheeks, smile into eyes.

"Darling Laura, how well you look!"

"What a becoming hat, child!"

"Laura, you look quite Spanish. I've never seen you look so striking."

And Laura, glowing, answered softly, "Have you had tea? Won't you have an ice? The passion-fruit ices really are rather special." She ran to her father and begged him. "Daddy darling, can't the band have something to drink?"

And the perfect afternoon slowly ripened, slowly faded, slowly its petals closed.

Initially Mansfield presents the party from the same distant angle from which she let us observe the gardener in the story's opening paragraph. From this more objective view, some details that we register at a peripheral level of consciousness are "[t]he band," "the hired waiters," "the marquee," "the flowers," and "the lawn." Mansfield's visual composition is one that subliminally reminds us of the role of the working people in producing this party. At the center, of course, are the "bright birds," trilling Kitty Maitland and the unnamed guests of the Sheridans; as Mansfield presents it and as the Sheridans have intended it to be, the party is a carefully constructed and managed surface of experience, even after the point-of-view angle shifts to a more personal level of exchange. That change, from omniscient height to Laura's place among the guests, is gradually and gracefully executed from the unanswered question "where?" down through the following sentence's clauses of increasingly personal experience, "press hands, press cheeks, smile into eyes." Without really noticing the magic of the transportation, we have floated from an upstairs window down into "the fray" with "Darling Laura." And what do the guests talk about in the few lines of dialogue that represent the whole of the party's chatter? Laura's hat now takes on a specific association with the party itself.

Laura carries herself with admirable modesty, her spoken remarks indicating her concern only for the pleasure of her guests, but from her "glowing," we (who know her so well by now) understand that vanity still has its hold on her and that the guests' compliments strengthen the hat's spell over her. We can hardly condemn her for finding it easy to be happy at the party rather than thinking about the dead man.

The party's end is rendered in Mansfield's musically and figuratively elegant one-sentence "petals closed" paragraph. The flowerlike "perfect afternoon" dispatches some dutifully remembering part of a reader's mind back through the story to the "literally hundreds" of roses and displaced daisies of the first paragraph, the sprig of lavender the workman "snuffed up," the abundance of canna lilies Mrs. Sheridan ordered, and perhaps even the gold daisies of Laura's hat. Flowers and garden parties, both perishable, are a luxury of the rich.

What do we feel about this much-anticipated and now terminated party? The text tells us that we are witnessing "happiness" and a "perfect afternoon." We hear the guests' departing compliments: "Never a more delightful garden-party…" "The greatest success…" "Quite the most…." Mansfield renders the beautiful surface of the experience in such a way as to make us intensely aware of the hollowness of it. The text explicitly encourages us to take satisfaction in the occasion, while implicitly evoking disappointment.

Here in its final moments, Mansfield directs us toward another kind of double perception by arranging a tableau:

> Laura helped her mother with the good-byes. They stood side by side in the porch till it was all over.

Once again we're reminded of the nature of work if you're a Sheridan—"the good-byes" are a duty so demanding that Laura must help her mother with them. Their standing "side by side" suggests a sameness in their relationship to this ritual, an equality of responsibility for it. Indeed, even though we've seen non-Sheridan tendencies in Laura, the likelihood is that as an adult she will take on a role very similar to that of her mother. All her upbringing—of which this party must be considered a part—is directed toward molding her into a version of Mrs. Sheridan. Interestingly enough, we didn't see Mrs. S. until the party was over, but just in case our impression of her personality might have faded from memory, she speaks up at this moment to remind us:

> "All over, all over, thank heaven," said Mrs. Sheridan. "Round up the others, Laura. Let's go and have some fresh coffee. I'm exhausted. Yes, it's been very successful. But oh, these parties, these parties! Why will you children insist on giving parties." And they all of them sat down in the deserted marquee.

This is the official Sheridan after-report of the event. This is what it means to be a Sheridan—exhausted from the successful carrying out of one's social obligations. Mrs. S.'s blaming the children for "insist[ing] on giving these parties" (when they and we know very well she has been the one who planned it in the first place and who refused even to consider Laura's suggestion that they call off the party) comes out of the same element of her personality that earlier caused her to accuse them of stealing the list of sandwiches from her bag. Though in both cases she speaks with her tongue in her cheek, this quality of her wit is nevertheless based on moral slippage. It's exactly the character-ingredient one needs to hold a garden party (with a band) while a new widow grieves just outside your garden gate.

Mentioning the marquee here reminds us of the workmen who came to put it up at the beginning of the day. Its now being deserted suggests the utter frivolity of erecting such a structure for an afternoon's pleasure. There's a witty appropriateness in that vision of all the Sheridans sitting out there under the absurd marquee; the thing adds a barely audible ironic resonance to the following conversation about the dead man:

> "Have a sandwich, daddy dear. I wrote the flag."
>
> "Thanks." Mr. Sheridan took a bite and the sandwich was gone. He took another. "I suppose you didn't hear of a beastly accident that happened to-day?" he said.
>
> "My dear," said Mrs. Sheridan, holding up her hand, "we did. It nearly ruined the party. Laura insisted we should put it off."
>
> "Oh, mother!" Laura didn't want to be teased about it.
>
> "It was a horrible affair all the same," said Mr. Sheridan. "The chap was married too. Lived just below in the lane, and leaves a wife and half a dozen kiddies, so they say."

With her teasing, Mrs. Sheridan demotes Laura back to the status of child at the same time she attempts to fend off the news of the death. And here again (as with the bread-and-butter and the cream puffs) Mansfield insinuates eating into a scene that contrasts the Sheridans with the working people. The Sheridans are luxuriously well-fed while in the garden patches of the working people "there [is] nothing but cabbage stalks, sick hens and tomato cans." Mansfield isn't really pleading the case of the working people, and she certainly isn't making a speech about a lack of economic justice. Her strategy is to make a reader share the assumptions of the Sheridans but also to be aware of these assumptions. Thus, each instance of eating has a charm to it. Instead of condemning such eating as we might if Mansfield's aims were more crudely polemical, we perceive it as the Sheridans themselves do: one simply does things this way. Here Mr. Sheridan's one-bite technique mildly amuses us because it is a masculine method of dispatching a femininely dainty party sandwich. Mr. Sheridan's bringing up the news of the dead man ("leaves a wife and half a dozen kiddies") echoes Godber's man's delivery of it some pages back ("left a wife and five little ones"). A true Sheridan, Mr. S. uses the approximate, rather than the precise, number of children.

In the two paragraphs that follow, Mansfield commits a breach of point-of-view etiquette by entering Mrs. Sheridan's consciousness:

> An awkward little silence fell. Mrs. Sheridan fidgeted with her cup. Really, it was very tactless of father...
>
> Suddenly she looked up. There on the table were all those sandwiches, cakes, puffs, all uneaten, all going to be wasted. She had one of her brilliant ideas.

Until this scene and after it, Laura is the only character to whose thoughts and feelings a reader has access. Occasionally the point of view angle has moved away from her and returned, but no other character has taken possession of the story by acquiring point-of-view status. When a new consciousness is encountered, a reader must make an adjustment in his or her perception of the world of the story, and so consistency of the limited-omniscient point of view has developed in modern narrative technique as a way of helping a reader focus on the flow of events. If there's a mistake anywhere in this story, it is in this violation of point-of-view consistency, and the damage from the temporary loss of focus is very slight. The workings of Mrs. Sheridan's mind might have been adequately conveyed by the following monologue:

"I know," she said. "Let's make up a basket. Let's
send that poor creature some of this perfectly good
food. At any rate, it will be the greatest treat for the
children. Don't you agree? And she's sure to have
neighbours calling in and so on. What a point to have
it all ready prepared. Laura!" She jumped up. "Get me
the big basket out of the stairs cupboard."

A reader makes several negative judgments about Mrs.
Sheridan's brilliant idea: the convenience of the gesture undercuts most of its moral value; one hears the false compassion of
"poor," the dehumanizing assumption of "creature," the smugness
of "the greatest treat," and the gloating of "What a point."
Nevertheless, a reader can't easily dismiss Mrs. Sheridan's
notion. Sending a basket of leftover party food would be a gesture
of some kind from the Sheridans to the dead man's family, and,
even in moral terms, this is better than nothing. It would probably
be exactly the kind of gesture the working people would expect of
the Sheridans. We readers have been shrewdly prepared to envision the working people's consideration and consumption of these
cream puffs that inspire "that absorbed inward look" and these
bite-sized sandwiches, but finally we have to admit that the food
will be eaten and appreciated by the people who live in "those
poky little holes." We're not confidently able to advise Laura as
she grapples with the issues:

"But, Mother, do you really think it's a good idea?"
said Laura.

Again, how curious, she seemed to be different from
them all. To take scraps from their party. Would the
poor woman really like that?

This is the only instance of Laura's consciously examining
how she might be different from the members of her family,
though by now the story has vividly demonstrated her

non-Sheridan tendencies. But here a reader notices both a difference and a similarity between Laura and her mother in seeing how Laura revises her mother's "poor creature" to the parallel but less condescending "poor woman."

Mrs. Sheridan's bullying her daughter's *thinking* is suggested by Mansfield's having Mrs. Sheridan respond to Laura's spoken question, "Do you really think it's a good idea?" only after Laura's interior monologue in which she has posed a more difficult question to herself, "Would the poor woman really like that?"

"Of course!" harps Mrs. S., so that she appears to be bulldozing Laura's delicate scruples, though she's actually responding to the easier question of whether or not it's a good idea to send the basket of food. Though a reader's impression is that Mrs. Sheridan has been grossly overbearing, Laura understands her mother, apparently doesn't take offense, and lets herself be persuaded:

> Oh well! Laura ran for the basket. It was filled, it
> was heaped by her mother.

"Oh well!" conveys some moral shrugging on Laura's part, some recognition of the ultimate sense of her mother's idea, but mostly recognition of the superior force of her mother's will. Here after the party's over, Laura is tired and unresisting. As a finishing touch of Sheridanism, Mrs. S. develops her idea one step further: "No, wait, take the arum lilies too. People of that class are so impressed by arum lilies." This last observation removes any doubts a reader might have had about Mrs. Sheridan's smug insensitivity.

But it's not just a matter of the mother's individually skewed values; it's the family ideology that's being articulated in these preparations to dispatch Laura through the gate with the basket. Practical Jose also has a contribution to make: "The stems will ruin her lace frock." Jose isn't quibbling over the impression the lilies will make on "[p]eople of that class"; she's playing the role of the big sister who's worried about Laura's dress, material goods and appearance obviously being the highest concerns of mature Sheridans.

A final breach of point-of-view etiquette—another entry into Mrs. Sheridan's consciousness—occurs in the following somewhat enigmatic passage:

> So they would. Just in time. "Only the basket then. And, Laura!"—her mother followed her out of the marquee—"don't on any account—"
>
> "What, mother?"
>
> No, better not put such ideas into the child's head!
>
> "Nothing! Run along."

About what does the mother mean to caution her daughter? What idea does she not wish to "put... into the child's head"? This question lingers in a reader's mind through the scenes that follow.

The beginning of Laura's journey is rendered in painterly terms with a deftly-shaded transition into Laura's introspection:

> It was just growing dusky as Laura shut the garden gates. A big dog ran by like a shadow. The road gleamed white, and down below in the hollow the little cottages were in deep shade. How quiet it seemed after the afternoon. Here she was going down the hill to somewhere where a man lay dead, and she couldn't realize it. Why couldn't she? She stopped a minute. And it seemed to her that kisses, voices, tinkling spoons, laughter, the smell of crushed grass were somehow inside her. She had no room for anything else. How strange! She looked up at the pale sky, and all she thought was, "Yes, it was the most successful party."

It is significant that she's journeying "down the hill" toward "where the man lay dead." "Down" and "darkness (or shadow)" are associated with death; "up" and "light" are associated with the party. Entirely to Laura's credit, she's able to articulate for herself the terms of her dilemma: "realizing" (an oddly precise word-choice: "making real for herself") the death of the man or remembering the party—and this opposition, death versus party, provides the basic tension of the entire story. But after she looks "up at the pale sky," her vacuously social phrasing, "Yes, it was the most successful...," invites us to see Laura in this moment as lost to Sheridanism at least temporarily.

The next paragraph parallels the previous one in moving through description to Laura's thinking, but it demonstrates both a more intensely affecting external world and a more vulnerable Laura:

> Now the broad road was crossed. The lane began, smoky and dark. Women in shawls and men's tweed caps hurried by. Men hung over the palings; the children played in doorways. A low hum came from the mean little cottages. In some of them there was a flicker of light, and a shadow, crab-like, moved across the window. Laura bent her head and hurried on. She wished now she had put on a coat. How her frock shone! And the big hat with the velvet streamer—if only it was another hat! Were the people looking at her? They must be. It was a mistake to have come; she knew all along it was a mistake. Should she go back even now?

The pattern of light and darkness is elaborated here, and the crab-like shadow is an ominous "realization" of the previous paragraph's "dog [that] ran by like a shadow." Laura's frock shines with a light that we must associate with the garden party. But the imagery is not simplemindedly symmetrical; remember, Laura's hat, the ultimate symbol of the party, is a black one. Even so, it makes her stand out distinctly in comparison with these working women wearing "men's tweed caps." Laura's anxiety here over her appearance and being looked at is augmented for us by our memory of Laura's self-consciousness around the marquee-installers, of the effect the hat had on her when she saw that "charming girl in the mirror," of how influenced she was by Laurie's telling her she looked "stunning" in it, and of the basic Sheridan obsession with matters of appearance. Although silly from an objective point of view, her doubts about her journey and her wondering if she should turn back seem reasonable enough to us. Instead of judging her from some distance, we are sympathetically with Laura on her journey, sharing her state of heightened self-consciousness when she reaches "the house."

> A dark knot of people stood outside. Beside the gate an old, old woman with a crutch sat in a chair, watching. She had her feet on a newspaper. The voices stopped as Laura drew near. The group parted. It was as though she was expected, as though they had known she was coming here.

The word *knot* conveys an ugly constriction—something Laura is feeling as well as something she is seeing. The image of a knot of people drastically contrasts her earlier description of the garden party where "there were couples strolling, bending to flowers, greeting, moving over the lawn."

As her innocent happiness of the morning transformed the Sheridan home into paradise, now Laura's fear has transformed her errand into a journey into the underworld. She departed through a gate; now she must arrive through another gate, this one guarded by a figure who must appear ominous to Laura, though the actual description of her ("old, old...with a crutch...watching...her feet on a newspaper") implies neither threatening nor benign qualities. The voices stopping and the group parting must also appear ominous to Laura, though again, to Mansfield's readers, they are neutral phenomena. That these people appear to have "expected" Laura, to have "known she was coming," is ambiguous in a way that enhances the scene: the clairvoyance is eerie, but in social terms to be "expected" is to be welcomed. Both these meanings are applicable to this moment of the story: because we know that Laura's carrying out her errand is the result of her mother's whimsy, we'd think it strange for the working people to have expected a Sheridan to convey the family's condolences to the dead man's family. It's likely that the group's "expectation" is for other visitors in general and that it is mostly imagined by Laura to be directed at her. In their silence and standing aside, the people are probably just responding politely and naturally to Laura in her party clothes. But in light of what we've seen of the social fabric of the culture—and especially of the working people's solicitous attitude toward the Sheridans—we can imagine that if one of them were dead, the working people would have made gestures of condolence to the Sheridan family. So it really isn't all that surprising. The ambiguity of Laura's reception marks a transition from her fearful journey down into the dark neighborhood into the oddly hospitable territory of the dead man's house—a hospitality felt more strongly by the reader than by Laura:

> Laura was terribly nervous. Tossing the velvet ribbon over her shoulder, she said to a woman standing by, "Is this Mrs. Scott's house?" and the woman, smiling queerly, said, "It is, my lass."

"Tossing the velvet ribbon over her shoulder" is Laura's attempt to play down both the garden party and the fact of her being a Sheridan. The woman's words, "It is, my lass," have that tone of kind deference that we first encountered in the lanky marquee-installer's "That's right, miss," but the queerness of the woman's smile serves to maintain the dark mood of the scene. Laura's level of anxiety remains very high:

Oh, to be away from this! She actually said, "Help
me, God," as she walked up the tiny path and
knocked. To be away from those staring eyes, or to be
covered up in anything, one of those women's shawls
even. I'll just leave the basket and go, she decided. I
shan't even wait for it to be emptied.

Does this circumstance call for prayer—especially when
we've seen no evidence of even the slightest spiritual concern in
the Sheridans' house? Well, no, it doesn't, and Mansfield's undercutting "actually" makes that clear to us. But since a scene soon
to come holds spiritual content, this little prayer is an unobtrusive
introduction of a spiritual *motif*. And even if her anxiety is merely
an acute case of self-consciousness, Laura's prayer conveys to us
the gravity she sees in her circumstance as she stands on the
threshold of the dead man's house.

Then the door opened. A little woman in black
showed in the gloom.
Laura said, "Are you Mrs. Scott?" But to her horror
the woman answered, "Walk in please, miss," and she
was shut in the passage.
"No," said Laura, "I don't want to come in. I only
want to leave this basket. Mother sent—"
The little woman in the gloomy passage seemed not
to have heard her. "Step this way, please, miss," she
said in an oily voice, and Laura followed her.

Both "gloom" (or "gloomy") and "passage" are repeated here,
and "passage" (a word with a neatly apt figurative application to
the scene) will reappear a few paragraphs later. Mansfield is moving Laura through the scene at a crisp pace; she's not about to
linger here in the hallway, but she is taking care to establish the
intensely claustrophobic qualities of the setting.

This is the third crone-like woman Laura has encountered at

the dead man's house (the other two being the "old, old [one] with a crutch" and the one who smiled "queerly." This third one will be Laura's escort in death's inner sanctum. Women are presiding over the ritual of death as earlier they presided over the garden party. And this woman, though she is kind and deferential in her manner, directs Laura, against Laura's wishes, to carry out what the woman deems to be the appropriate behavior for the occasion. Laura's encounter with the marquee-installers at the beginning of the story has prepared us for her encounter with this woman. A reader could imagine Jose saying, "No, no, I'll just leave this basket with you," and turning back toward home. But since Laura let the men put up the marquee in front of the karakas trees, helped her mother with the sandwich flags, accepted the hat from her mother, and stopped arguing against holding the garden party, we certainly don't expect her to disobey this woman. Mansfield has established malleability as essential to Laura's character, and it is against her will that Laura carries out this last stage of her journey. It would be against any Sheridan's will to go farther than the front door of the dead man's house. Indeed, we might now suspect that the warning Mrs. Sheridan meant to give Laura was "don't on any account go into that house." The difference between Laura and all the other Sheridans is that she has it in her character to defer to this lower class woman. On the one hand, we see her acting out of her democratic impulse, out of basic human decency; on the other hand we wish she had a little more backbone. Although we understand that she is the only Sheridan who's capable of carrying this journey to its conclusion, her weakness is what prevents us from seeing her as excessively good, her actions as overly noble. The odd combination of weakness and courage in her actions now is a fresh dimension of Laura's character for this late section of the story. But Mansfield is taking care to show Laura to be "better" than the other Sheridans only to the extent that she is more wholly human.

She found herself in a wretched little low kitchen lighted by a smoky lamp. There was a woman sitting before the fire.

"Em," said the little creature who had let her in. "Em! It's a young lady." She turned to Laura. She said meaningly, "I'm 'er sister, miss. You'll excuse 'er, won't you?"

"Oh, but of course!" said Laura. "Please, please don't disturb her. I—I only want to leave—"

But at that moment the woman at the fire turned round. Her face, puffed up, red, with swollen eyes and swollen lips, looked terrible. She seemed as though she couldn't understand why Laura was there. What did it mean? Why was this stranger standing in the kitchen with a basket? What was it all about? And the poor face puckered up again.

"All right, my dear," said the other. "I'll thenk the young lady."

By reverting to her mother's phrasing with "wretched little low kitchen" and "the little creature," Laura is staving off her fear. And Mansfield isn't romanticizing her portrait of the lives of working people: the lamp is "smoky," and the widow's name (or as much of it as we're able to hear) is one crude syllable. Nor is Mansfield romanticizing Laura's response to the situation; the girl is blurting the absolute truth when she says, "I only want to leave." The personality of the widow's sister, the "little creature," emerges unobtrusively in her speech; like Godber's man, she appears to be savoring this death. The power of the widow's grief is made evident by her silence—in stark contrast to her sister's obsequious utterances—and by Mansfield's explicit description of her face. The effect of that description is intensified by Mansfield's having described no one's face until this moment. We're seeing the widow's face through Laura's eyes, and the effect of it on Laura is to inspire a leap of empathy: Laura imagines the widow's impression of her, so that in this moment, visually and emotionally, both characters sharply register in a reader's consciousness. Laura and the widow can't bring themselves to speak to each other, but the widow's sister is intent on performing the manners called for by the occasion:

> "All right, my dear," said the other. "I'll thenk the young lady." And again she began, "You'll excuse her, miss, I'm sure," and her face, swollen too, tried an oily smile.

If Laura's reading of the widow's face is at all accurate, then with "All right, my dear," the widow's sister is merely pretending to be in communication with her; in spite of her own grieving (her face is "swollen too"), she is doing her best to carry out what she sees as suitable behavior. Em's sister is the only character in the story we hear using such dialect as "thenk," "'er," and "'e," though we heard a "yer" from cook and a "matey" sung out by one of the marquee-installers; even though the story is so much about class-differences, Mansfield uses lower-class dialect with a very light hand. But in this scene, this is the third time "swollen" and the second time "oily" have been used, their effect being to deepen our sense of Laura's revulsion at her circumstance:

> Laura only wanted to get out, to get away. She was back in the passage. The door opened. She walked straight through into the bedroom, where the dead man was lying.

Although inconspicuous, this is an artful paragraph. We're aware of Laura's emotional condition, and so we understand how, when she's "back in the passage" (that word again), she'd assume that an opening door would take her back outside. That this door opens without visible human agency must be attributed to Laura's nightmarish state of mind. And either "the passage" is a different one or the door that opens is not the door that Laura entered earlier—Mansfield deliberately does not clarify which is the case, but it doesn't matter because we understand that Laura is disoriented anyway. So intensely do we feel her desire to escape that we understand how she can take several steps into the bedroom before she realizes she's "where the dead man was lying"; Mansfield's syntax saves the dead man for last, and so we come upon him with a surprise similar to Laura's. A considerable complexity is conveyed by this thirty-one word paragraph.

Mansfield has established and developed this minor character of Laura's escort for a number of reasons, not the least of which is that she serves as a kind of ambassador for the community outside the Sheridans' gate; Laura has more interaction with this woman than with any other working-class character in the story. The widow's sister is also here for purposes of tone and pacing and for the dramatic highlighting of this moment. She is also the one character in the story who can credibly make this presentation of the dead young man. After "the little creature" accomplishes the task, she disappears from the story.

> "You'd like a look at 'im, wouldn't you?" said Em's
> sister, and she brushed past Laura over to the bed.
> "Don't be afraid, my lass,—" and now her voice
> sounded fond and sly, and fondly she drew
> down the sheet—" 'e looks a picture. There's nothing
> to show. Come along, my dear."

The relish Godber's man took in telling the story of this man's death has prepared us for Em's sister's fondness of voice and gesture in "showing" the dead man. That "'e looks a picture" calls to a reader's mind Mrs. Sheridan's earlier manipulative flattery of Laura, "I have never seen you look such a picture." This woman's comforting "There's nothing to show" is her delicate way of telling Laura that the man's body has not been visibly damaged by the accident that killed him. Her final words, "Come along, my dear," have the ominous-seductive ring of the wolf's voice in "Little Red Riding Hood."

The ritual that's being performed here is remarkable; "the little creature" may be a minor character, but in this moment, she's a high priestess. She is initiating Laura in the mystery of death; she's also showing Laura a man, as an object or specimen; she's allowing the girl "a look" of greater thoroughness and intensity than she has likely ever been able to have of any living man—because she doesn't have to feel self-conscious while she's looking. Death of course is the primary thematic element here, but the scene is also charged by romantic and erotic undercurrents. In the same way that Mansfield's not having previously described anyone's face gives special emphasis to her description of the widow's face, her not having previously given men any more than passing attention now adds dramatic force to Laura's encounter with this man.

Of more interest than the last two-word paragraph we encountered ("Sadie went") is "Laura came." It conveys Laura's following an order, just as Sadie followed one. Throughout the story we've seen Laura carrying out the will of others, doing almost nothing of her own accord. A reader imagines that she feels torn by the invitation; probably she both wants and doesn't want "a look," but Mansfield is telling us nothing of her thinking and feeling. Another writer might have seen Laura's decision—to look or not to look—as the very crux of the story, but Mansfield doesn't linger an instant because she sees the next moment as the crucial one:

> There lay a young man, fast asleep—sleeping so soundly, so deeply, that he was far, far away from them both. Oh, so remote, so peaceful. He was dreaming. Never wake him up again. His head was sunk in the pillow, his eyes were closed; they were blind under the closed eyelids. He was given up to his dream. What did garden-parties and baskets and lace frocks matter

to him? He was far from all those things. He was wonderful, beautiful. While they were laughing and while
the band was playing, this marvel had come to the
lane. Happy… happy…. All is well, said that sleeping
face. This is just as it should be. I am content.

Instead of being the horrifying sight a reader expects, the dead
man is, through Laura's view of him, "wonderful, beautiful," a
sleeping fairy-tale prince. But the source of the young man's beauty is not his physical appearance; it is his being dead. Laura is
seeing through the young man to his death, which she interprets
as a dream; death is a "marvel" to her because it is so remote from
the worldly "fray" of "garden parties and baskets and lace
frocks." The "Happy… happy" here calls to a reader's mind, from
five pages back, "Ah, what happiness it is to be with people who
all are happy, to press hands, press cheeks, smile into eyes."
Laura's romantic vision is at work in constructing both these
worldly and spiritual versions of happiness, but the story presents
the latter as a "truer happiness." To Laura, the dead man's body is
a revelation of his spirit that "is given up to his dream." With the
happiness of the garden party, a reader was directed to be skeptical by the social chit-chat that follows the assertion of it ("Darling
Laura, how well you look!" "What a becoming hat, child!"). But
here a reader is directed not entirely to disregard the happiness
death offers by the fact that Laura is alone with her thoughts and
feelings. Through Mansfield's excessively positive language, we
understand Laura's response to the dead man to be romantically
exaggerated, but we don't feel that response to be completely
invalid—just as we don't feel that her democratic impulses
are invalid. A relevant ambiguity is at work in this "extravagant"
diction ("wonderful, beautiful… marvel… Happy"); it is at one
and the same time garden-party chit-chat and the language
of awe. While Laura is probably the only Sheridan capable of
experiencing awe, she's nevertheless stuck with the Sheridan

vocabulary for articulating it even to herself. Almost as a way of protecting the truth she has received from the dead man, Laura remembers her manners and agrees with herself to put on an act for him:

> But all the same you had to cry, and she couldn't go
> out of the room without saying something to him. Laura
> gave a loud childish sob.
> "Forgive my hat," she said.

The hat here reverberates back through the story, so that silly as it sounds for Laura to ask forgiveness for her hat, we understand her actually to be asking forgiveness for her entire life. Her hat is her identity as a Sheridan, as a vain creature, as a person devoted only to worldly matters. The truth of the spirit is what she has witnessed in the dead man, a truth that stands in direct opposition to the worldly values with which she has been raised. A reader's response to Laura's plea for forgiveness is to laugh—what an absurd thing for her to say!—but we have been so instructed by the story that another part of what makes us laugh is our shock in apprehending the profundity of the moment. On the backlash of understanding, we know that nothing Laura could say would be as meaningful and correct as "Forgive my hat."

These words have a cathartic effect. They release the pressure the entire story has directed toward Laura's encounter with the dead man. Now Mansfield quickens the pace for Laura's escape:

> And this time she didn't wait for Em's sister. She
> found her way out of the door, down the path, past all
> those dark people. At the corner of the lane she met
> Laurie.
> He stepped out of the shadow. "Is that you, Laura?"
> "Yes."
> "Mother was getting anxious. Was it all right?"
> "Yes, quite. Oh, Laurie!" She took his arm, she

pressed up against him.

"I say, you're not crying, are you?" asked her brother.

Laura shook her head. She was.

However profound her encounter with the dead man has been, the Sheridanesque phrasing of her perception of "all those dark people" demonstrates that Laura has not been transformed by it into a completely new person. In fact, her escort back to her own world is that Sheridan most like herself, her soul-mate brother. Having just carried out a spiritual exchange with the dead man, she responds to the living Laurie by "press[ing] up against him," a phrase that echoes the garden party's happiness in the form of "press[ing] hands, press[ing] cheeks." Laurie's phrasing of his question suggests the official Sheridan surprise at—and perhaps disapproval of—crying over a dead workman; Laura, in shaking her head to deny her crying, accepts that view, though the amusingly contradictory next sentence ("She was") reflects the complex truth of her tears: they are not out of sorrow over the workman's death; they are the tears she brought forth as a performance for the dead man, but she has nevertheless gone on crying. So we know that even though Laura is going back to her house and her worldly life as a Sheridan, she has been deeply affected by her spiritual experience in the dead workman's house. What remains for the story to tell us?

Laurie put his arm round her shoulder. "Don't cry," he said in his warm, loving voice. "Was it awful?"

"No," sobbed Laura. "It was simply marvellous. But, Laurie—" She stopped, she looked at her brother. "Isn't life," she stammered, "isn't life—" But what life was she couldn't explain. No matter. He quite understood.

"*Isn't* it, darling?" said Laurie.

On the surface of it, this is certainly a happy ending, a moment of affection and rare understanding between brother and sister. But it is also an ending that invites us to scratch that surface and to reconsider the whole story in light of its final vision. Laura's "It was simply marvellous" is a tri-faceted pronouncement: 1) it has that Sheridanesque ring of garden-party chit-chat, 2) it's an odd thing to say about an encounter with the dead, and 3) it lightly touches the reader's memory of the bedside scene ("while the band was playing, this marvel had come to the lane"). Under scrutiny, the happiness of the final vision considerably diminishes: the understanding between Laura and Laurie, as they phrase it here, is resounding testimony to their need—an essential of Sheridanism—to stay entirely on the surface of "life." In beginning to phrase her question, Laura essays bravely toward some kind of truth, but she lets herself be too easily stopped by Laurie's response. All of their training—as we have seen it demonstrated throughout the first three-quarters of the story—prevents Laura and Laurie from having a real exchange about anything of consequence, let alone matters of mortality. Indeed, one of the echoes of Laura's stopped observation in this passage is her mother's warning ("And, Laura!"—... "don't on any account—"), a warning that specifically might have been against entering the dead man's house, or perhaps even against looking at the dead man's body, but that in general terms might have been something like "don't on any account penetrate the surface of experience."

Closer examination of this passage darkens the ending's vision still further: there is a hollowness to this brotherly understanding suggested by the two previous brief scenes in which we have seen Laurie. Remember, just before the party, Laura wanted to tell him about the accident that killed the workman, but by complimenting her appearance in the hat, he prevented her from even starting to tell him. The sentence "He quite understood" is Laura's thinking, but we readers have been taught to see very little capacity to understand in Laurie's character. And after all,

123

even if he were a brother of unusual sensitivity and depth of character, how could he understand the remarkable moments Laura experienced at the dead man's bedside? So what the ending demonstrates beneath its cheerful warmth is Laura's essential isolation. Earlier in the story we witnessed her wrongly thinking that Jose would understand her and then that her mother would understand her; the argument of the story is clearly that the Sheridans can't comprehend Laura's non-Sheridan qualities. The complex shading of Mansfield's prose has insinuated a disturbing perception into the deeper levels of a reader's consciousness: a sensitive, spiritually-inclined young woman is so trapped within her delusions that she can't "realize" how isolated she is within her family.

Laura Sheridan participates in the preparation for and giving of a party, then journeys into a slum where she briefly encounters a dead man before she starts to walk back home. By themselves, the events of "The Garden Party" are of only mild interest and small consequence. However, when invested with the subtle power of Mansfield's style, the account of these events takes on force, complexity, and substance: a life we come to understand as remarkable is shown at a crucial point of development. Style does all the work; the way this story is told is the story; "The Garden Party" would be no story at all without the fine shading of Katherine Mansfield's prose.

7 ON RESTRAINT:
Advice for the Promiscuous

She picked up a photo album and went carefully through it—musing for hours about the smiles that covered the faded pages. The book had pictures of Lizzie from infancy until she was about fifteen. After that, Lizzie had usually been successful in her ardent duckings from the camera. Marilyn sipped at a glass of vodka during her reminiscence. Her eyes widened at pictures of the family together. Winston, Marilyn, and Lizzie—grinning through extravagant vacations, highly celebrated birthdays, and present-laden Christmases. Marilyn now realized that the pictures meant nothing—the poses were just as inane as Lizzie had professed the day she tried to throw the book away.

Marilyn slammed the album back in place and solemnly walked into the kitchen. It was late and Lizzie hadn't returned. Marilyn put the dinner and dishes and food away. She wasn't hungry. She began to walk back into the living room and stopped short as the grandfather clock clanged disturbingly—ten horrible times. The heavy front door eased open and Lizzie appeared.

Neither woman said anything. Marilyn noted every movement her daughter made. Lizzie looked hard into her mother's eyes and turned sharply. She kneeled on

the plush gold couch and molded her long, white fingers around the shaft of the silver pistol. Marilyn stood
slightly drunk and very dumbfounded. Lizzie moved
soldier-like and halted directly facing her mother.
Marilyn couldn't respond. Her thin lips quivered silently. Before her, Lizzie cocked the gun thunderously.

When the daughter finally spoke, it was with severe
clarity and purpose. Her lines resounded, like those
practiced by an actress. "Feel me bleed, Mother," she
demanded, inserting the pistol into her hollow, white
temple. "Taste the thickening, red slime as it hardens
on my screaming wounds. See that the stench of death
mourns only the enduring life. I need to sleep. I need
to die."

Lizzie pulled the trigger and exploded her skull into
the room. Marilyn recoiled as Lizzie's juices splattered
on her dress and dribbled down the beige walls. Blood
gurgled in pulsing waves from Lizzie's shredded, gaping head. The body lay still in its horror—except for
the final convulsions of Lizzie's free fingers—tap, tap,
tap—on the floor. And then the dead silence.
Winston's plaid beret had been disturbed from its position on the brass coat-rack; it lay meekly on the
floor—approached by the widening red pool.

Marilyn stood mutely in wonder of the scene as it
quietly thundered in her mind. The phone incessantly
jangled the hard silence, somewhere in the back-
ground. Marilyn felt clumps of rage swell and clutter
her throat. She staggered forward—wanting to escape.
But her limp legs faltered and she fell to the slippery,
reddening wood floor. Groping, her hands met those of
Lizzie's—cold and sticky with the terrible death.
Marilyn's senses blurred and she vomited violently.

Finally she groveled to the door, leaving horrible red finger prints where she passed.

The tragic figure weaved into her car and lurched out of the garage. She recklessly scraped across the side of her husband's Mercedes during her exit. The long, red clawings shown distinctly against the flawless, silver finish.

Marilyn thrust her anger through her feet to the accelerator and sped away. She might have been a wax figure in a museum—rigidly fixed in her position. Her shock white skin was darkened by two fiercely deadened eyes. But her mouth appeared alive. Her lips moved, seemingly uttering a noiseless tirade. They stopped suddenly, displaying a grotesque, enduring smirk.

Flyaway Curve became visible in the distance through the smudged windshield. Marilyn's head bobbed slightly—as if acknowledging a friend. "I've always loved you, Lizzie," Marilyn tenderly murmured as the accelerator touched the floor. The red metal swerved and cut smoothly and swiftly through the feeble barricade. Then Marilyn and her car leapt and fell and flew away, into the deep bottom of the canyon.

The story from which this passage is taken came to me in an advanced class at a good, expensive school with a serious creative writing program. Its author had finished at least two semesters of creative writing before he enrolled in my class. I would like to say that his story is unusual, and that I seldom encounter writing like this. But I can't. If I teach another twenty-five years, I will probably receive another twenty-five versions of the Marilyn and Lizzie story. I invite the reader to consider the appropriate teacherly response to such work.

One option might be to tell the student that the story proved conclusively that its author had no talent for writing and that the student should never again attempt to write fiction. That response would certainly serve the art of fiction-writing, and it might save the student the drawn-out pain of gradual disillusionment. It might backfire, and the student would become more determined than ever to become a novelist or story-writer. Most likely the student would complain to your department chairman or dean: "My teacher criticizes only negatively."

But let's say that Murphy's Law has been temporarily suspended in this situation and things go exactly as they should. You tell the student he ought never to try writing another story. He looks relieved, tells you he'd been getting more and more interested in his accounting courses, tells you he tried the creative stuff only because his dad forced him to. He whips out a form already filled in so that he can drop your course and take Macroeconomics. You initial the form, the kid shakes your hand, thanks you, then pauses at the door. He turns and gives you this sincere look and says, "Uh, just for my own good, could you tell me what's wrong with that garbage I wrote and how I might have corrected it." Now what are you going to tell the kid? Nothing's at stake. You've already informed him that the writing stinks, and he agrees with you that it does. Now can you describe the problem with that writing? Can you tell the student how he might correct that problem?

The writing in the Marilyn and Lizzie story lacks restraint. By *restraint*, I mean decorum, control, a holding back, a measuring of language against silence. The word *restraint*, in this sense, describes an esthetic morality: the artist will do certain things but will not do certain other things; the artist will say some things but will not say some other things.

In the Marilyn and Lizzie passage, we can feel the absence of restraint. We sense that this writer will hold nothing back, will say anything, will do anything. So the problem with this student's writing is esthetic promiscuity.

That promiscuity informs the relentless dramatic progress of the story. In two pages two characters die violently, the mother grovels in the daughter's blood, and so on. We can feel that promiscuity in the melodrama of what these characters are made to say: "Feel me bleed, Mother," "I've always loved you, Lizzie." We can sense that promiscuity in the bulldozing diction that's at work in almost every sentence: "Marilyn *recoiled* as Lizzie's *juices splattered* on her dress and *dribbled* down the beige walls. Blood *gurgled* in *pulsing waves* from Lizzie's *shredded, gaping* head."

We ought to ask ourselves what's wrong with esthetic promiscuity. My answer is that it won't yield the truth. We feel nothing solid over there on the writer's side of the prose, no conviction, no engagement with the real issues of the situation, no effort to do anything other than make an impression. Reading this story is like holding a conversation with someone you know is lying to you: characters are being manipulated, and some extravagant diction is being offered up, but the mouth has been taken right out of these words.

We can say how this writing makes us readers feel while we're reading it, and we can speculate about what's going on with the writer while he's working at this passage. But what about IT, the thing on the page? What's wrong with it?

Danger is a basic ingredient of all stories, even the ones in which nothing dangerous ever occurs. I think of Katherine Mansfield's "The Daughters of the Late Colonel" as one of the most genteel stories I know, one in which the two main characters, Con and Jug, are these immensely fragile ladies to whom nothing terrible ever happens; as the story proceeds we are made to feel how very dear these ladies are and how utterly unequipped they are to live in the world. But they're not harmed. They're never even seriously threatened by anything or anyone. And yet danger plays its role in the story; it holds the story under a kind of pressure, enlivens it, sharpens and vivifies the events, the characters, the language.

It is my opinion that most story-writers become adept at measuring out danger in their stories, but that good story-writers will always exercise restraint, will often allow violence to enter their stories but will seldom allow danger to become wholly realized. In a good story the worst that can happen will never happen. That holding back helps engage a reader's attention, helps keep a reader involved in the story. If the worst that can happen happens, then a reader is released from participating in the story. Oh God, it happened, there isn't anything I can do, I might as well stop thinking about these people and these events and this world. At the end, the Marilyn and Lizzie story is as interesting as a limp balloon, a balloon that was blown up and then let go to fly wildly about the room whooshing and farting out its air.

We could tell the author of the story that to correct the problem, he would need to revise with the aim of adding restraint to the language and drama of the story. We would be advising the promiscuous to become chaste. But let's assume the student is willing to accept that advice and wants to see how somebody else did it. Here's one of the most violent scenes I know in a short story. It's from Caroline Gordon's "The Captive," in her *Collected Stories*, a narrative of a pioneer woman captured by Indians:

> Then we started back to the house with the milk.
>
> We were halfway up the path when we heard the Indians holler. We started for the house on a dead run. I could see Indians in the yard and one Indian was coming around the house to the back door. I ran faster and slipped in the door ahead of him. Joe was right behind me. The room was so full of Indians that at first I couldn't see any of my children. The Indians was dancing around and hollering and hacking with their tomahawks. I heard one of the children screaming but I didn't know which one it was. An Indian caught me around the waist but I got away from him. I thought, I

had got to do something. I fell down on my knees and crawled around between the Indians' legs, they striking at me all the time, till I found Martha, my littlest one, in the corner by the loom. She was dead and I crawled on a little way and found Sadie. She was dead, too, with her skull split open. The baby was just sitting there holding on to the bar of the loom. I caught him in my bosom and held him up to me tight; then I got to my feet. Joe was right behind me all the time and he stood up when I did. But an Indian come up and brained him with a tomahawk. I saw him go down and I knew I couldn't get any more help from him. I couldn't think of anything to do; so I worked my way over toward the door, but there was two or three Indians standing on the porch and I knew there was no use running for it. I just stood there holding the baby while the Indians pulled burning logs out of the fire onto the floor. When the blaze had sprung up they all come out onto the porch.

I made a break and got some way down the path, but an Indian run after me and caught me....

...I kept looking back toward the burning house, thinking maybe they wasn't all dead before the Indians set fire to it. Finally I couldn't stand it no longer and I asked the old Shawnee. He pointed to one of the young Indians who was going up the ridge ahead of us. I saw something dangling from his belt and I looked away quick. I knew it was the scalps of my children.

A number of deaths—say, approximately five—occur in one paragraph here, and so my student might rightfully exclaim, "This is an example of restraint?" I'd try to make my case, first of all, on the basis of the diction: we do have *hacking*, *screaming*, *skull split open*, *brained*, and *scalps*. But given the circumstances of an

Indian raid, that's a pretty spare gathering of words of violence. And compare them to what we can find in two sentences of Marilyn and Lizzie: juices *splattered, dribbled, gurgled, pulsing waves, shredded, gaping*.

In the second place, I'd make my case for restraint in this passage by citing at least two other aspects of the scene that the writer deems of more importance than the horror of the events. The first is voice. Gordon cares about character more than horror here, and so she uses the flat diction of Jinny Wiley's voice even though that diction will not richly conjure up the terror of this scene. What it will register is Jinny's courage, resourcefulness, and practicality, her frontierwoman's toughness. The second important aspect here is the chaos, of which the horror is one part. Many things are happening around Jinny Wiley, all of them registering in her consciousness. Details are selected carefully, but the point-of-view camera doesn't linger any one place; we pass from Martha to Sadie to the baby to Joe very quickly and then out to the porch. The effect here is one of measuring out the direct violence to which the reader is exposed. The result is that when we come to the last sentence I've quoted, "I knew it was the scalps of my children," the horror is momentarily focused so that a reader registers something of the devastation that Jinny Wiley must feel in seeing what she sees. This is a gory passage of prose, but the most violent aspects of the scene are those imagined by the reader on the basis of the details provided by the writer. Because we readers do the imagining from a phrase such as "the scalps of my children," the horror registers with us much more intensely than it would if the author showed us every "final convulsion." Because we do that imagining, we are engaged in the world of the fiction, whereas in Marilyn and Lizzie we don't have to participate, and so our response is to distance ourselves, mentally and emotionally getting the hell away from there.

If we go by statistics, then the six deaths in Flannery

O'Connor's "A Good Man Is Hard To Find" must rank that story very high among the violent stories of our literature. O'Connor's management of that violence is exemplary. The murders of Bailey, John Wesley, June Starr, the baby and the mother occur "back in them woods," as the Misfit calls it. The reader hears the pistol shots while the Misfit and the grandmother hold their theological conversation. Once "There [is] a piercing scream from the woods followed closely by a pistol report," and in terms of diction, "piercing" is perhaps the most violent moment of the story. The one murder we are shown directly, that of the Grandmother, is presented in such chaste language that it appears to be an only slightly violent incident:

> She saw the man's face twisted close to her own as if he were going to cry and she murmured, "Why you're one of my babies. You're one of my own children!" She reached out and touched him on the shoulder. The Misfit sprang back as if a snake had bitten him and shot her three times through the chest. Then he put his gun down on the ground and took off his glasses and began to clean them.
>
> Hiram and Bobby Lee returned from the woods and stood over the ditch, looking down at the grandmother who half sat and half lay in a puddle of blood with her legs crossed under her like a child's and her face smiling up at the cloudless sky.

Once the grandmother has been shot, we readers realize that the other five members of the family have also been shot. Of course we've been hearing the pistol shots from the woods, and we heard that "piercing scream." But we hoped all along that they weren't really being killed, that they would come walking out of those woods at the end. That hoping is one significant way we are involved in the story. The effect on us of the final murder does not need to be emphasized by the author. In fact O'Connor's final description of the grandmother, "her legs crossed under her like a child's and her face smiling up at the cloudless sky," is directed against the grain of the horror of what has happened. This management of violence is connected to one of the central ironies of the story, that the grandmother, in her obsession with worldly matters—being a lady, having good blood, and so on—gives up her real family, sacrifices them, lets them be murdered without really even giving them her full attention. And we readers, in our desire for the terrible not to happen, collaborate with the old lady in that sacrifice. When the Misfit finally does force the Grandmother toward her moment of spiritual insight, it comes in the form of spiritual adoption, her seeing the Misfit as "one of [her] own children." The amount of restraint involved in managing the violence of "A Good Man Is Hard To Find" is enormous, and so is the impact of the story on a reader. Violence has served the author's thematic concerns so thoroughly that even though almost the worst that can happen has happened, a reader continues to think about the story, to try to unravel its levels of meaning. The moment of grace and spiritual insight that the Grandmother has just before her death complicates everything, continues to hold the story under pressure, and keeps the reader engaged with the world of the fiction.

The presence of danger is a major element in J. D. Salinger's "A Perfect Day for Bananafish." In the first section, we learn that Muriel's mother is concerned for her daughter's safety in the presence of the bizarrely behaving Seymour, but their telephone conversation is so funny that we don't worry too much about Muriel's plight. In the second section we worry momentarily that Seymour may sexually molest the little girl, Sybil Carpenter:

> "Sybil," he said, "you're looking fine. It's good to
> see you. Tell me about yourself." He reached in front
> of him and took both Sybil's ankles in his hands.

But then it becomes immediately clear that Seymour won't do

that; instead he teaches Sybil a funny and useful lesson about being cruel to animals. Then again we worry—at a very low level of anxiety—that maybe Seymour is going to drown Sybil:

> He kept pushing the float. The water was not quite up to his chest. "They lead a very tragic life," he said. "You know what they do, Sybil?"
>
> She shook her head.
>
> "Well, they swim into a hole where there's a lot of bananas. They're very ordinary-looking fish when they swim *in*. But once they get in, they behave like pigs. Why I've known some bananafish to swim into a banana hole and eat as many as seventy-eight bananas." He edged the float and its passenger a foot closer to the horizon.

But we're quickly relieved of that anxiety:

> He took Sybil's ankles in his hand and pressed down and forward. The float nosed over the top of the wave. The water soaked Sybil's blond hair, but her scream was full of pleasure.

After Seymour kisses the arch of Sybil's wet foot, they say goodbye, and we readers have been charmed by how innocent, how tender Seymour has proven himself to be. If Seymour is a mad man, we feel, then all of us should be blessed with such madness.

The fourth section of the story quickly disillusions us when Seymour accuses the lady in the elevator of looking at his feet:

> "I have two normal feet and I can't see the slightest God-damned reason why anybody should stare at them."

This is crazy behavior, and it is mildly violent, enough so that we are prepared for the final paragraph of the story, even though we're still strongly under the influence of the tender Seymour-and-Sybil section. Here are the final two paragraphs of the story.

135

He got off at the fifth floor, walked down the hall, and let himself into 507. The room smelled of new calfskin luggage and nail-lacquer remover.

He glanced at the girl lying asleep on one of the twin beds. Then he went over to one of the pieces of luggage, opened it, and from under a pile of shorts and undershirts he took out an Ortgies calibre 7.65 automatic. He released the magazine, looked at it, then re-inserted it. He cocked the piece. Then he went over and sat down on the unoccupied twin bed, looked at the girl, aimed the pistol, and fired a bullet through his right temple.

Syntax is the main instrument of violence-management in this paragraph. Not until the final three words do we know that Seymour is committing suicide. The story has set up a dynamic so that we expect him to shoot the sleeping Muriel. Her phone conversation with her mother has revealed her to be worldly and insensitive. (We're reminded of that earlier scene by the smell of "new calfskin luggage and nail-lacquer remover.") Seymour's bananafish safari with Sybil has shown him to be a kind of saint of sensitivity. The episode in the elevator has shown Seymour to be capable of rage. It stands to reason that he would shoot Muriel, and we readers participate in the story, watching Seymour prepare to do this terrible thing that we don't want him to do but that we expect he will do. That he shoots himself instead of Muriel is in no way less horrible, but it requires us to reconsider the whole story, look at everything again. In this case the danger has been present in the story from the very beginning, and it has been one of the main forces compelling us through the story. That the danger is not realized until the final three words is an extremely austere presentation of violence in fiction.

So far I have been extolling the virtues of restraint in fiction-writing. I believe that restraint is a sign of what I've called esthetic morality, an unwillingness of the artist to indulge in excess. I believe that restraint makes "better" fiction because it involves—indeed it requires—more reader participation, more intense engagement with the world of the fiction. I could stop there. I've shown my student author of the Marilyn and Lizzie story what's wrong with his writing, and I've shown him some examples of writers who have handled similar situations with restrained writing. But I'm uncomfortable with leaving it at that. What this amounts to is advising the writer to be cautious, to be measured, to hold back. Well, yes, we've seen that such advice does apply to some awfully good writing. But couldn't it also be the case that caution, measuring, holding back, would result in some dreadfully unexciting fiction? Isn't the ultimate example of restrained writing the dullest story ever written: He went to the store. He bought a loaf of white bread. He came home. He felt better. (And maybe I should cut that bold adjective, "white.")

Viewed this way, *restraint* takes on a negative connotation: restriction, limitation, a closing down of possibility, being tied down, being denied freedom.

Peter Taylor is a writer I admire a great deal. As an undergraduate at the University of Virginia, I studied under him, and I dearly love a good dozen or so of his stories. But I think he's too restrained sometimes. Here are the paragraphs that mark the turning point of Taylor's "At the Drugstore":

> "My father," [the young pharmacist] said quietly, "suggests that you probably ought to see a doctor."
>
> Matt understood at once that there was more than one interpretation that could be made of that message. "I believe I'd like to speak to the pharmacist myself," he said, and was already striding alongside the counter and toward the doorway to the prescription room. But the young Conway was moving at the same speed behind the counter. They converged at the entrance to

Mr. Conway's prescription room. And simultaneously the figure of the old druggist was framed in the doorway. Matt went up on his toes and peered over Mr. Conway's shoulder! He saw it all, the white cabinets and the bottles and the long work shelf, all so like a hundred other pharmacists' shops he had had passing glimpses of. Everything about it looked so innocent and familiar and really quite meaningless. There was no satisfaction in it for him at all—not even in the glass of water which he identified as the receptacle for Mr. Conway's teeth. But what kind of satisfaction should he have got? he asked himself. What had he expected? Something inside him which a moment before had seemed to be swelling to the bursting point suddenly collapsed.

"You told my father you were in a hurry," he heard the young pharmacist say. "I think you'd better get going now." Looking at the young man, Matt observed that he definitely had a nervous tic in one eye. And all the blood had gone out of his cheeks now. He was in a white rage. Why, he even had his right fist tightened and was ready to fight Matt if necessary to protect the old druggist. The incredible thing was that only a moment before, Matt himself would have been willing to fight. Why? What had possessed him? Already the whole incident seemed unreal. Surely he had been momentarily insane; there was no other way to explain it. He backed away from the two men, turned his back to them, and quickly left the drugstore.

The idea behind this story seems to me admirable: an ordinary man works himself into an extraordinary state of mind on a trip to the drugstore. This passage doesn't seem to me to reflect bad writing. What's wrong with it, for me is that it just isn't enough. I want more from the central events of a story than these paragraphs offer me. More what? I want to feel a greater intensity of experience. Taylor needs that exclamation point after the phrase "peered over Mr. Conway's shoulder!" He needs it because the reader wouldn't feel any intensity at all without the punctuation mark there to direct him. And the "all" that is seen here, the innards of the prescription room, is simply not enough to satisfy my hunger for something remarkable in a story.

I believe that a single-minded holding to the principle of restraint will lead to dull writing. I believe, furthermore, that restraint is a teachable quality of writing and therefore is the sort of value that graduate writing programs might emphasize beyond the point where the value is valuable. Restraint can be taught in many cases through editing, cutting unnecessary modifiers, substituting more precise verbs, eliminating gratuitous details, and so on. Such teaching and learning certainly ought to be accomplished. But restraint is not an absolute value.

In fact, some of the most thrilling moments in literature seem to me to have come out of a writer's having broken through the normal limits of restraint. Which is to say that the author holds this esthetic morality, this code of things he will and will not do in his writing, but that he comes to a point in the writing of his story where he simply must break his own rules. To write his story he must do what he ordinarily would not do. The first example that comes to mind of such a moment in recent fiction is in D. M. Thomas's *The White Hotel*. The novel allows an extraordinary intimacy to develop between the reader and the main character, Lisa Erdman; the structure of the novel allows a reader to see Lisa from various angles, to know her at various levels of thought and feeling, to take on the whole complicated "self" of this other human being; Lisa Erdman becomes very dear to a reader. And then in the fifth section of the novel, Lisa and her adopted son are murdered with thousands of others in the Nazis' massacre at Babi

Yar. The passages rendering the massacre, the murders, and the immediate aftermath are written with masterful objectivity; restraint manages the violence in such a way as to make reading that part of the novel a disturbing experience. As it should be. But in the final pages of that section, at the point where the old woman who is Lisa "seemed to have stopped breathing," both reader and author have been brought to such extremes of sorrow and outrage that something is required that goes beyond restraint, beyond the rules of fiction. Thomas breaks off the section and breaks loose from the given point of view:

> During the night, the bodies settled. A hand would adjust, by a fraction, causing another's head to turn slightly. Features imperceptibly altered. "The trembling of the sleeping night," Pushkin called it; only he was referring to the settling of a house.

> The soul of man is a far country, which cannot be approached or explored. Most of the dead were poor and illiterate. But every single one of them had dreamed dreams, seen visions and had amazing experiences, even the babes in arms (perhaps especially the babes in arms). Though most of them had never lived outside the Podol slum, their lives and histories were as rich and complex as Lisa Erdman-Berenstein's. If a Sigmund Freud had been listening and taking notes from the time of Adam, he would still not fully have explored even a single group, even a single person.

> And this was only the first day.

Beginning with the quotation from Pushkin, one can feel the author entering the fiction with his own voice to express the indignity he feels over the events he has just described, to shake his fist at the sky. *The White Hotel* is a sophisticated, complex work; except in this one instance, it is an extremely controlled novel. But a reader feels grateful for this passage; what Thomas

expresses here needed expressing. The fiction called for a breaking through the limits of restraint, and the technical flaw of this
authorial intrusion is considerably outweighed by the overall thematic and emotional balance of the section.

In *Black Tickets*, Jayne Anne Phillips has written some powerful contemporary short shorties; Phillips's work is significant, I
think, because she explores the limits of restraint. She writes can-
didly about sexual experience. She is able to make beautiful stories out of material we might once have thought unsuitable for
respectable fiction. Here's a passage from her most sensational
story, "Lechery," whose narrator is an orphaned fourteen year old
girl who seduces young boys:

> I do things they've never seen. I could let them
> touch but no. I arrange their hands and feet, keep them
> here forever. Sometimes they tell me stories, they keep
> talking of baseball games and vicious battles with their
> friends. Lips pouty and soft, eyes a hard glass glitter.
> They lose the words and mumble like babies; I hold
> them just so, just tight, I sing the oldest songs. At times
> their smooth faces seem to grow smaller and smaller in
> my vision. I concentrate on their necks, their shoulders.
> Loosen their clothes and knead their scalps, pinching
> hard at the base of the head. Maybe that boy with dark
> hair and Spanish skin, his eyes flutter, I pull him across
> my legs and open his shirt. Push his pants down to just
> above his knees so his thin legs and smooth cock are
> exposed; our breathing is wavy and thick, we make a
> sound like music. He can't move his legs but stiffens in
> my lap, palms of his hands turned up. In a moment he
> will roll his eyes and come. I'll gently force my coated
> fingers into his mouth. I'll take off my shirt and rub my
> slick palms around my breasts until the nipples stand
> up hard and frothy. I force his mouth to them. I move my

141

hand to the tight secret place between his buttocks.

Sometimes they get tears in their eyes.

Some readers may find the sexuality of this passage offensive in the same way that the violence of the Marilyn and Lizzie story is offensive. Some readers may feel that the author is throwing the stuff out to try to make an impression. My opinion is that this passage is much closer to the Caroline Gordon paragraphs from "The Captive." The diction is overtly sexual, but it is controlled; we find no excessive verbs, no piling up of modifiers. The voice of the character is of more importance than any of the details. And the overall effect of the tableau—the way they sit with the girl controlling the boy as if he were a doll—is the main thing this passage conveys.

This is pure speculation on my part (though perhaps I could make a strong case for it by discussing all of the stories in *Black Tickets*), but I believe Jayne Anne Phillips has as strong a sense of restraint as any of the good writers I've mentioned so far. But I believe she pushes herself to go beyond those limits. I believe she does it to gain access—and to give us readers access—to kinds of experience we have not heretofore known about. A very good student of mine found the story "Lechery" offensive because, she said, the writing reflected no desire on the part of the author to change the circumstances that made this narrator become what she has become; the writing seemed to her to cherish, to savor the life this child lives. My own notion is that this writing informs us about this life, makes us feel it deeply; that accomplishment seems to me of more value than a number of social rehabilitation programs. That accomplishment seems to me to have come only out of a purposeful going beyond the boundaries of good taste and conventional attitudes about sex, the poor, the underprivileged, and the very young. It also seems to me to come out of a purposeful going beyond the limits of restraint in fiction-writing—the kind of restraint that might demand that we present such scenes through suggestion, that we draw such a tableau by way of the reader's imagination, not so directly, so boldly.

But restraint had to be there in the first place for the going beyond restraint to have been possible. Jayne Anne Phillips had to have that sense of esthetic morality in order for her disregard of it to have any significance and in order for her to write the scene effectively, to write it beautifully. The writing has an extra charge, or intensity, as a result of its having come forth in spite of Phillips's reticence, its having broken through the pressure of Phillips's restraint.

When I think of this combination of restraint and the willingness to put restraint aside for the sake of the story, I think immediately of John Cheever. One of his earliest stories, "Goodbye, My Brother," was overwhelmingly concerned with manners and nuances of speech, but at its center was this thrilling moment of primitive violence:

> "You're a gloomy son of a bitch," I said. "You're a gloomy son of a bitch."
>
> "Get your fat face out of mine," he said. He walked along.
>
> Then I picked up a root and, coming at his back—although I have never hit a man from the back before—I swung the root, heavy with sea water, behind me, and the momentum sped my arm and I gave him, my brother, a blow on the head that forced him to his knees on the sand, and I saw the blood come out and begin to darken his hair. Then I wished that he was dead, dead and about to be buried, not buried but about to be buried, because I did not want to be denied ceremony and decorum in putting him away...

And of course there is the famously outrageous final sentence of "The Country Husband," one of Cheever's most suburban stories:

> Then it is dark; it is a night where kings in golden
> suits ride elephants over the mountains.

In Cheever's work there is a sweetness and a playfulness in
his disregard of the "rules" of fiction-writing. He was a man who
at the end of his life argued that "a page of good prose is invinci-
ble," and he was certainly able to write page after page of impeccable prose. But he was also an impishly clever boy who liked
demonstrating how much fun it was not to obey the rules—and in
so demonstrating called attention to how much of writing has to
do with the rules and playing around with the rules. The whimsical moments of his stories seem to me to match, not accidentally,
the whimsical moments of what we understand to be our "real
lives." There are two such unrestrained moments in "The World
of Apples," the story of the troubled poet, old Asa Bascomb. The
first moment is at the end of Bascomb's worst day, one in which
"He simply wrote F—k again and again covering six or seven
sheets of paper.... He started down through the vineyards to the
main road at the bottom of the valley":

> As he approached the river a little Fiat drew off the
> main road and parked among some trees. A man, his
> wife, and three carefully dressed daughters got out of
> the car and Bascomb stopped to watch them when he
> saw that the man carried a shotgun. What was he going
> to do? Commit murder? Suicide? Was Bascomb about
> to see some human sacrifice? He sat down, concealed
> by the deep grass, and watched. The mother and the
> three girls were very excited. The father seemed to be
> enjoying complete sovereignty. They spoke a dialect
> and Bascomb understood almost nothing they said.
> The man took the shotgun from its case and put a sin-
> gle shell in the chamber. Then he arranged his wife
> and three daughters in a line and put their hands over
> their ears. They were squealing. When this was all

arranged he stood with his back to them, aimed his gun at the sky, and fired. The three children applauded and exclaimed over the loudness of the noise and the bravery of their dear father. The father returned the gun to its case, they all got back into the Fiat and drove, Bascomb supposed, back to their apartment in Rome.

The second unrestrained moment is part of a healing dream Bascomb has toward the end of the story:

> It was an old, small, poor country church. The angel was in a chapel on the left, which the priest lighted. The image, buried in jewelry, stood in an iron cage with a padlocked door. The priest opened this and Bascomb placed his Lermontov Medal at the angel's feet. Then he got to his knees and said loudly: "God bless Walt Whitman. God bless Hart Crane. God bless Dylan Thomas. God bless William Faulkner, Scott Fitzgerald, and especially Ernest Hemingway." the priest locked up the sacred relics and they left the church together.

What seems to me "unrestrained" about these moments in "The World of Apples" is that they come out of nowhere, they are gratuitous. They are extra-logical in terms of the story's dynamics. But then once they are in place and part of the story, they become necessary. A reader cannot imagine the story without these deliciously improbable moments in it.

My conclusion is a paradox, one that seems to me certain to convince my student lingering in the doorway to find out what was wrong with "Marilyn and Lizzie" that switching over to Macroeconomics is the best thing for him to do. What I have to tell him is that he must incorporate the rules and regulations of *restraint* into his writing, he must take on esthetic morality. And then he must learn how to set aside those rules and regulations,

145

must learn how to go beyond esthetic morality. He must learn restraint. Then he must learn to ignore restraint. I don't wonder about when he gives me a final skeptical look and walks on down the hall, shaking his head, leaving me alone in my office. He is doing the right thing.

8 PUTTERING IN THE PROSE GARDEN:
Prose Improvements for Fiction-Writers

oday's conventional wisdom, particularly around graduate writing programs, is that what a young fiction-writer must do to achieve success is find his or her own voice. "Finding one's own voice" has a nobler sound than "trying to sell a few stories," and I suppose that, to the extent that it's too vague a notion for anybody to do anything much on the basis of it, the idea itself is harmless. My concern is that it may discourage some young writers from carrying out work essential to their apprenticeship. One can do what one pleases in the name of trying to find one's own voice, or do nothing in the hope that one's own voice will suddenly arrive, like a lightning bolt to the throat. I'd like to suggest a more practical approach for serious story-writers and novelists.

In the fiction I read nowadays, I find four categories of prose, and I think of them on a kind of evolutionary scale of development.

Basic Prose is an honorable category. The writer of it can use language in a correct and acceptable manner. It is the minimum level of performance for any fiction-writer who hopes to have any success at all. But many aspiring fictioneers (which is to say, students paying tuition to graduate writing programs) haven't mastered it. There are two distinguishing features of Basic Prose, the first of which is not particularly interesting: its correctness. One often feels that writers of Basic Prose are probably language bigots; they wince if you split an infinitive or end a sentence with a preposition; they hate it when you say "hopefully." Correctness is what matters. But it is the second distinguishing feature that is the crucial one in thinking about the consequences of Basic Prose: language has no particular connection to subject matter. As we go up the evolutionary scale in categories of prose, we find that the relationship between language and subject matter deepens, intensifies. But at this level, language and subject matter, though together on the page, don't have anything to do with each other. Here's an example of Basic Prose, the first paragraph of a novel published by W. W. Norton & Company in 1968:

> If a man's name is not Bormann or Beck or Mueller, but once was, the month of May has a double significance in history. For it was in May that a war never to be surpassed in ferocity—if civilization is to survive on this planet—ended in Europe. And in a May twenty years later a special kind of justice began to grind to a halt. This was the justice of the law books, which trailed the Bormanns and Becks and caught some of them and sent them to prison for crimes against humanity. It did not catch them all, and as the May debate on the German Statute of Limitations ended, pseudonymous men in hiding places all over the world began to breathe a little easier. In Bonn and Mannheim and Dusseldorf for a few more years the courts will be picking at the last ugly threads of the concentration camp cases and tying them up in neat packages and stamping them with official seals. But for the most part, the purge is over.
>
> —Bynum Shaw
> *The Nazi Hunter*

The reader of this passage is being told about experience without being given much of a feeling for it. There may be a kind of stylishness here (consider, for instance, the syntax of the first

148

sentence), but it is a style willed into being by the author without adequately considering content. Functionally weak, this style is all authorial ego.

Window-Pane Prose is not only an honorable category, it is also a desirable one. Here language is utterly functional. Language is on the page only for the purpose of allowing the reader access to the experience of the fiction. This language is modest. It may be graceful language, but it never calls attention to itself. It stays out of the way. Here are examples, first paragraphs of stories by two distinguished contemporary story-writers:

> The campus security guard found her. She wore a parka and she lay on the foot-bridge over the pond. Her left cheek lay on the frozen snow. The college was a small one, he was the only guard on duty, and in winter he made his rounds in the car. But partly because he was sleepy in the heated car, and mostly because he wanted to get out of the car and walk in the cold dry air, wanted a pleasurable solitude within the imposed solitude of his job, he had gone to the bridge.
>
> —Andre Dubus
> "Townies"
> *Finding a Girl in America*

The house was not itself. Relatives were visiting from the country. It was an old couple this time, an old couple who could not sleep after the sun was up and who began yawning as soon as dinner was over in the evening. They were silent at table, leaving the burden of conversation to their host and hostess, and they declined all outside invitations issued in their honor. Cousin Johnny was on a strict diet. Yet wanting to be no trouble, both he and cousin Annie refused to reveal any principle of his diet. If he couldn't eat what was being served, he would do without. They made their own beds, washed out their own tubs, avoided using salad forks and butter knives. Upon arriving, they even produced their own old-fashioned ivory napkin rings, and when either of them chanced to spill something on the table cloth, they begged the nearest Negro servant's pardon. As a result, everybody, including the servants, was very uncomfortable from the moment the old couple entered the house.

—Peter Taylor
"Guests"
Happy Families Are All Alike

Window-Pane Prose is usually just as correct as Basic Prose (though its correctness is not as visible), but Window-Pane Prose gives a reader immediate and clear access to the experience of the story. Language is wholly at the service of subject matter. Window-Pane Prose writers depend on the human drama to carry their stories; their discipline is a particularly saintly one: they must be so fluid, deft, and precise that no one notices their work, the making of the sentences through which the reader "sees" the story.

Personable Prose is language with a definite personality, and that personality becomes a part—usually a somewhat small part—of the story. Sometimes we think of the personality of the prose as the "voice" of the author. More often we think of it as connected with the personality of a character in the story. One of the main advantages of Personable Prose is that the reader will be attracted to the personality of the language. I suppose it is possible for a reader to be put off by the personalities of some proses, but in the case of a writer like J. D. Salinger, a reader is usually so charmed by the language that he fails to notice some of the story's short-comings (mushy philosophy, for instance). It's probably fair to say that Personable Prose is the largest category of writing by successful American story-writers. Here are two examples, again first paragraphs of stories:

When he was eighteen and was leaving home for the first time, Ralph Wyman was counseled by his father, principal of Jefferson Elementary School and trumpet soloist in the Weaverville Elks Club Auxiliary Band, that life was a very serious matter, an enterprise insisting on strength and purpose in a young person just setting out, an arduous undertaking, everyone knew that, but nevertheless a rewarding one, Ralph Wyman's father believed and said.

—Raymond Carver
"Will You Please Be Quiet, Please?"
Will You Please Be Quiet, Please

We are a family that has always been very close in spirit. Our father was drowned in a sailing accident when we were young, and our mother has always stressed the fact that our familial relationships have a kind of permanence that we will never meet with again. I don't think about the family much, but when I remember its members and the coast where they lived and the sea salt that I think is in our blood, I am happy to recall that I am a Pommeroy—that I have the nose, the coloring, and the promise of longevity—and that while we are not a distinguished family, we enjoy the illusion, when we are together, that the Pommeroys are unique. I don't say any of this because this sense of uniqueness is deep or important to me but in order to advance the point that we are loyal to one another in spite of our differences, and that any rupture in this loyalty is a source of confusion and pain.

—John Cheever
"Goodbye, My Brother"
The Stories of John Cheever

Whereas Window-Pane Prose gave us clear access to the

experience of its story, Personable Prose pulls us closer to the experience by exposing us immediately to personality. The relationship between the reader and the story is a more intimate one.

Mega-Prose is extremely heightened language, language of greater density and energy, more pronounced rhythmic qualities, richer textures of sound. Mega-Prose aims for intensity. Mega-Prose, like Personable Prose, reflects personality, but in this case personality has been souped up. The quality of mind it reflects is quickness, allusiveness, quirkiness, liveliness in general. Here are four examples:

> Iactura vigoris non fortuita est: agitur semper unum antitetrahedron. This dust of poppy, fitchet, bone is in an exact precession with which the gods are intimate but not our rough minds. Who, seeing a mother on her knees before the mammillaria of Cybebe, the Arvals flouring a calf for the knife, the standards of Quirinus in white mist around the watchfires, could believe that the gods are as indifferent as gravity. I huddle upon the wild rose, wait with the moth upon the wall, still as time.
>
> —Guy Davenport
> "C. Musonius Rufus"
> *Da Vinci's Bicycle*

> Here it is sweltering. Claire wears the diaphanous and Josie (I have seen) rolls her shorts to sausages, airs those legs all across town. I fan. I think. Listen to droplets fall from Momma's air conditioner in her lair above the garage. *Gnats should festoon such a love as mine.* He's written on vellum, "How could *my* hard heart matter when love is itself a diamond set in bone?" Which I tell Claire, floating in, saying,

"Rhythmically, you know, such care, I swear it cools the insides of my arms."

—Eve Shelnut
"Descant"
The Formal Voice

Talmudic scholar, master of cabala, Isaac felt vulnerable to a thousand misfortunes in New York, slipped on an icy street, lay on his back and wouldn't reach for his hat. People walked, traffic screamed, freezing damp sucked through his clothes. He let his eyes fall shut—no hat, no freezing, no slip, no street, no New York, no Isaac—and got a knock against the soles of his shoes. It shook his teeth. His eyes flashed open, darkness spread above him like a predatory tree, a dozen buttons glared and a sentence flew out, beak and claws, with a quality of moral sophistication indistinguishable from hatred: "What's-a-matta, fuckhead, too much vino?" He'd never heard of vino, but had a feeling for syntax—fuckhead was himself. He said, "Eat pig shit," the cop detected language, me-it became I-thou and the air between them a warm, viable medium. He risked English: "I falled on dot ice, tenk you."

—Leonard Michaels
"Isaac"
Going Places

Blind people got a hummin jones if you notice. Which is understandable completely once you been around one and notice what no eyes will force you into to see people, and you get past the first time, which seems to come out of nowhere, and it's like you in church again with fat-chest ladies and old gents gruntin a hum low in the throat to whatever the preacher be saying. Shakey Bee bottom lip all swole up with

Sweet Peach and me explainin how come the sweet-potato bread was a dollar-quarter this time stead of dollar regular and he say uh hunh he understand, then he break into this *thizzin* kind of hum which is quiet, but fiercesome just the same, if you ain't ready for it. Which I wasn't. But I got used to it and the onliest time I had to say somethin bout it was when he was playin checkers on the stoop one time and he commenst to hummin quite churchy seem to me. So I says, "Look here Shakey Bee, I can't beat you and Jesus too." He stop.

> —Toni Cade Bambara
> "My Man Bovanne"
> *Gorilla, My Love*

When we began at the bottom of the evolutionary scale with Basic Prose, we found that the facts of the situation of the story were coming to us as we needed them: we understood the situation, we just didn't know what it felt like. Here at the top of the scale with Mega-Prose, we find ourselves in situations—all four of these examples, by the way, are beginning paragraphs of stories—where *we know what things feel like before we understand them.* Mega-Prose plunges us so deeply and so immediately into experience that much of what we're doing when we're reading is trying to figure out what the hell is happening in the story. This is the ultimate degree of intimacy between reader and story: the reader has been pulled so far into the story that he is struggling to see the outside of it. If it works, Mega-Prose involves a reader more wholly than the other Proses. Not only does the reader "get" more of the experience of the story, the story also "gets" more of the reader.

"If-it-works" is a shadow that hovers over most stories written in Mega-Prose. It's brittle stuff, and it's hard to make it yield a narrative. My response to Mega-Prose is usually that I like it if, and in direct proportion to, the sense I can make of it. I'm willing to travel some distance through a story in a state of confusion, but after a while I want to be able to start adding things up. So my liking for the four examples is in ascending order: my desire to go on reading is weakest in the Davenport paragraph and strongest in the Bambara.

In setting forth these categories as a set of steps, I do not mean to be suggesting that we story-writers try to work our way up to the top and all of us become Mega-Prose writers. I don't think the world is ready for a stampede of Mega-Prosers.

But if Basic Prose is the only kind I can write, then, yes, I do need to improve myself. There are NO good stories in which there is not some relationship between the language and the experience of the story. The minimally acceptable relationship is that of Window-Pane Prose. If I'm a Basic Prose writer, then I should try writing Window-Pane and/or Personable. In both these latter categories, I'm required to give myself over to the story, as opposed to making the story submit to the one kind of prose I can write. And this "giving oneself over" to the material is one of the big secrets, it seems to me, of writing good stories.

If I write only one or two of the "acceptable" kinds of prose, then I should try to write the kind or kinds that I don't write. For different kinds of stories, a writer will need different kinds of instruments. More stories are available to the writer who can use different kinds of prose. To "stretch" seems to me good advice for any writer at any stage of development, and it also seems to me advice that is in direct contradiction to the notion of "finding your own voice."

It is true that we can see and hear distinctive qualities of language in the work of certain writers, and those qualities are what we might call "voice," or "style." But that kind of voice, or style, is something that, in my opinion, no good writer ever tried for or thought very much about. Style comes so much from the center of personality that it is present, or not present in one's writing in the same way that personality itself is present or not present, authentic or artificial, in every walking-around human being. Though it is commonly thought to be so, conscious refinement of style is not the key that will unlock the power of good writing.

The story-writer whose work seems to me exemplary here is Eudora Welty. Almost every Welty story has a different quality of language. In "Powerhouse," she's writing Mega-Prose, in "Why I Live at the P. O.," she's writing Personable Prose, and in "A Worn Path," she's using a wonderfully clean Window-Pane Prose. Because she can write various kinds of prose, she can handle various kinds of material. How could a young, middle-class white woman write so exuberantly and convincingly about the lives of Black Jazz musicians in "Powerhouse"? The power is in the language, in the author's giving herself over to the language of the subject.

So much of the luck of writing depends on uncontrollable forces that even the most arrogant of writers are humble in the face of the work to be done. Style, in that it is, in the deepest sense, *personality*, comes out of these uncontrollable forces. Your best writing is your best self, for better or for worse. That idea is frightening because it may turn out that your best self is not somebody intelligent, wise, generous, sensitive, or honorable enough to make literature. But the idea is also comforting because your best self is the only legitimate resource you have to bring to your writing. You don't have to try to guess what your readers want you to be writing, what sort of style would be most appealing to them. Who you are is what they get, and they can take it or leave it.

It is helpful to remember that the writer works for the story— works for the work. If you can let go of self-esteem, self-protection, self-concerns of various sorts, including the selfish concept of the sacredness of "your own voice"—if you can let go of all that, then you can work *with* the work. The work itself will commence a kind of dialogue with you. Once you kick out that passage of grand writing (in which perhaps you felt "your own voice" take flight) and try to find what the story needs to replace it, the story itself can begin instructing you: Look, you began this way, and obviously this is your ending—don't you see what you're getting at? The language itself has powers, and what a prose-writer needs to do is not to seek control over those powers but to find ways to open him- or herself up to them. To find yourself working with the work, collaborating with the language, these are the highest pleasures of the prose garden.

9 MYSTERY AND METHOD:
Writing's Mundane Journey
toward the Mystical

Page one, upper left hand corner! my sarcastic high school band director used to shout at us. Beginning is purely mechanical. Set down a word, follow it with another, still another, and so on. I have so little difficulty with beginnings that I produce probably ten or twelve times as many of them as I do completed pieces of writing.

But somewhere along the way—somewhere in that sequence of one word following another—a mysterious exchange of energy must begin to occur between the writer and the piece of writing. I've never gotten over the first surprise I felt when something I was writing took on such a life of its own that it began drawing patterns and perceptions from me that I hadn't known were within me. At the time, I must have thought that here was a power I would learn to control. But the fact is that a fair portion of my writing continues to seem "beyond me"—beyond my wisdom, intelligence, or complexity of soul. And many of my writing efforts, lacking that exchange of energy, come to nothing whatsoever. When I write something and learn nothing from it, that's a sure sign the piece has failed. It is still the case that when I do achieve good work, it almost always seems an undeserved gift, something that has come to me in the process of one word following another, aside and apart from my effort and ability. Whatever that power is that enables me to transcend myself through my writing, I've never learned how to summon it at will.

What I have learned to appreciate most about that power is that it won't be controlled. When I have it, I'm happy as a gambler on a winning streak. When I don't have it, I yearn for it soon to come back to me.

At the age of 47, after more than twenty years of commitment to the literary craft, I think I've finally figured out several working-methods that allow me more regularly to receive and use that power when it chooses to come my way. These methods have become so essential to the health of my writing life that I can't believe somebody didn't mention them to me early on in my apprenticeship.

The first of these fundamentals is that to avoid distractions in my writing time, I need to use my non-writing time to take care of matters that might break my concentration (concentration being basic for anyone who wishes to tap into art's mysterious energy).

What sorts of things interfere with a writer's concentration? Letters are high on the list—nothing is so attractive to a fiction-writer with a difficult scene to write as that old pal who's been owed a long letter for months. But bills, too, and balancing one's checkbook, and all of those financial and household "naggeries," as I've come to call them: If I can't pay all my bills (as is usually the case), then what I have to do is stash them someplace where they won't catch my eye. And straightening up; I amaze myself with my ability to leave my desk untidy all day long, then when I have finally captured a quiet hour or two, suddenly I must use that sacred time for tidying up my desk—and my study, too, while I'm at it and in a mood for squaring things away. A friend of mine mopped her kitchen floor at one in the morning so that she wouldn't be tempted to do it after she'd slept and wanted to go straight to her writing.

Any rational person could figure out such a principle: take

care of correspondence, bills, neatening up the work-area, and all other petty details during non-writing hours, so as to be able efficiently to use writing hours for writing. Contrary to popular belief, most writers are extremely rational people—to figure out a next sentence or line of poetry requires a basic aptitude for cause-and-effect. But there is a certain point in my daily life when I just don't think straight.

Every morning, when I sit down to write, I suddenly don't want to write. I can be deeply immersed in my material, fascinated by my characters, full of optimism that *this* will be the best thing I've ever written; I can be up early and feeling good, feeling proud of myself for having brilliantly disposed of every possible distraction to my writing; I can have my glasses cleaned and my coffee cup and my back-up thermos full and my computer and printer humming at my fingertips and my hours of free time open right there before me and nothing else pressing to do, when suddenly I just don't want to write.

I think of this obstacle to my writing as a small psychological membrane that must be pierced each morning. I'm a little bitter about it. Now that I have made that (in many ways absurd) commitment to giving myself over to the written language on a daily basis, it is clearly unfair that I still have to put up with this silly difficulty.

But the Suddenly-Not-Wanting-To-Write-Writer's-Syndrome (SNWTWWS) is an inescapable fact. I'm certain it has cost me many a page of writing. Before I learned the necessity of clearing away distractions from my writing time, it would usually get the best of me unless I had something that I urgently wanted to get down on the page.

Recently, though, with the assistance of computer technology, I've developed a sly technique for dealing with SNWTWWS. Ritual is the key. The first steps of my ritual are elementary and obvious: I turn on my computer and open my file. The next step is only slightly challenging: I have to find the place in my document where yesterday I started writing "from scratch"—where yesterday's new writing began. The final step is the hardest, but even this one is not truly difficult. I simply have to start editing yesterday's new writing. It's an easy assignment, an invitingly do-able task, fifteen minutes—maybe a half hour at most—of sharpening the phrasing, cutting the fat, and filling in the chinks, a warm-up just to get the old diction and syntax muscles limbered up.

But the result of this little ritual of going-over my previous day's work is that when I reach the end of that task, without even thinking about it, I'm generating new writing. I'm absorbed in making something out of language. I wouldn't dream of quitting now that my concentration is focused and my energy has been released into the work.

Swimming is my metaphor for this phenomenon of outsmarting SNWTWWS: whereas the idea of diving into the cold water can sometimes put me off swimming altogether, if I start out by wading into the warm shallows, before I know it, I'm swimming and having a hell of a fine time.

What about those occasions when I don't have any old writing to go over at the beginning of my writing day? Well, now that I've caught on to outsmarting SNWTWWS, I find that I almost always have some old writing to go over. My ongoing circumstance is one of having lots of writing projects all at once, some of them just begun, others in second and third drafts, still others needing only a bit of polishing before I pronounce them finished.

This particular essay, for instance, was begun on a morning when I'd just finished adding pages 417 and 418 to the novel manuscript I've been working on for the past year. Before this draft of my novel will be finished, I have another 75 or so pages to write; in this essay, I have another eight or nine pages to go; I have a chapter of my novel that I've lifted out and begun to convert into a short story; I've got some finishing touches to put on the manuscript of a story that's already been accepted by a journal and some more polishing to do on a long essay for a textbook; I have a manuscript for a new collection of poems that needs about a year's worth of pruning, filling in, tinkering, and rearranging: it's endless. If I began nothing new and concentrated only on finishing up my current projects, I'd still have two or three years' worth of revising to keep me busy.

So I anticipate that there will never be a time when I don't have some old writing around that needs to be gone over. That's the case because I've come to understand I need old writing around to jump-start my new writing. I've also come to depend on this layering method of composition as the one best suited to my inclinations and circumstances. I've figured out how to manipulate my habits in order to get the most out of myself.

One of my habits that I've gotten better and better at manipulating is that of choosing what I'll work on first in any given morning. What I've come to understand is that contrary to my natural inclination, I have to work on my most important project first, or I'm not likely to work on it at all. My natural inclination is to tackle the easiest available task first—say, a manuscript that needs just a few words changed and maybe a new paragraph inserted and/or an old one deleted. My natural inclination is to evade the writing that will require my greatest effort, but that's the work that needs my best energy. So some of what I do while I shower and shave and arrange my writing day in my mind is to lock into place the order in which I'm going to address the things I want to accomplish for the morning. For the past year, my novel has been what I've had to struggle to keep as my highest priority, though (tricky me) I've tried to distract myself with stories, poems, and essays. Those pieces of writing have their place in my overall schedule, but for most mornings of this year they haven't been getting my absolutely primary resources.

Figuring myself out has been a not insignificant part of making a productive writing life. From my days of being an eager graduate student, I remember hounding my teachers about one thing and another, desperate, really—though I guess I didn't know it at the time—for an answer to the looming question of how I was ever going to get my writing done. Knowing what they knew, my teachers were kind and patient with me. But I wasn't able to hear them when they tried to tell me their version of the answer: you have to construct your writing life around your own inclinations, resources, and circumstances.

Of one thing I'm certain: not one of the eleven writing teachers I studied under ever suggested that I try to imitate the way he or she did things. Even though in this very essay I'm offering up my own methods for consideration, I nevertheless admire my teachers for not having done so. I think they understood all along what I've learned only through years of trying to maneuver myself toward more and better writing, that along with the writing itself, a writer must create his or her own methods for getting it done.

Creating the methods goes on and on. A few habits remain constant, but I can't just construct a complete system and stick to it. What worked last year goes a little stale this year. Instinctively I make changes: for a few months, I'll be working with my laptop in the living room, then I'll go back up to my attic study and my regular computer. Or for the music I need for companionship while I work, I'll be listening to Bach's Cello Suites for a week or two, then I'll have to hear Jim Hall and Red Mitchell, or Rigoletto, or Mahler, or Emmylou Harris...

No matter how much I tinker with my system, there is always room for improvement. My current project is that of trying to conquer First-Wind Wimp-Out (FWWO). I've established a routine of getting up early, sitting down to my keyboard, piercing SNWTWWS, and generating a page or two or three each morning. But not every piece of my writing happily submits to such suburban methods. There are plenty of mornings when I sense that the impending scene is one that is going to demand more of my time and energy than I'm accustomed to giving out. FWWO encourages me to quit early, before I get into the heavy stuff; or once I'm into it, FWWO whispers to me that I've got no business trying to write this big scene with what little energy and concentration I have left. FWWO suggests that I need to stand up and stretch. FWWO reminds me that more coffee is available in the kitchen and probably something to eat, and while I'm there FWWO reminds me that the trash needs to be taken out, and so on.

FWWO is SNWTWWS's little cousin, not as overtly destructive but ultimately more subversive for my writing. In fact more than one critic—friendly and otherwise—has pointed out an unsettling emotional evenness to my writing. Some of that evenness has to do with my esthetic principles—I count myself among those writers who honor restraint. But some of it also has to do with the fact that working only two or three hours a day on my writing prevents me from losing myself in its emotional momentum the way I might if I were able to work five or six hours at a stretch.

So what am I doing to build up resistance to FWWO? This is a tough problem, because the methods available for dealing with it (so far as I've yet found) aren't easily ritualized. What I have to do is try to raise my level of patience through artificial stimulation. For instance, on my desk, I keep certain toys (a marble, a small carved bloodhound, a furry bird-like finger-puppet) designed not to destroy my concentration but to offer me a mild break through tactile or visual play. My best toy is a smooth, oval, black rock that my hands take pleasure in rubbing while I stare at my computer screen.

But to keep sitting at my keyboard, I quite often have to start sweet-talking myself: *Stay here just a little longer. You've got all morning to go get that cup of coffee. Here, change the syntax in this sentence. And look here, you can be more specific here. And hey, this character has her hand resting on something—what is it? The toaster oven? My god, won't she burn herself?*

With monologues and interrogations that direct me back into the task at hand, I have to distract myself from my distractions. The guiding principle of such mental coaching is short-term involvement. If I promise myself that I have only to stretch my attention span the slightest little bit, often I'll again become engaged in the vision of the piece, writing maybe another hour or so before I realize how I've tricked myself.

These gyrations of the consciousness seem to me peculiar to the task of writing. With most other kinds of work, there are tangibles that must be dealt with—paint, pipes, lumber and nails, destinations, hearings, stock, phone calls, etc. But an uncontracted piece of writing may remain incompletely suspended forever; with no one else caring or even knowing about it, its creator may cease work at any point—mid-chapter, mid-paragraph, or even mid-sentence. Writing is the most gossamer of tasks. Until it is finished, its maker must suffer doubts about the metaphysical validity of a piece of writing.

Having something begun but not finished brings forth a certain kind of anxiety in me. I am pained by doubts of my ability to finish it and by doubts of its value even if I do finish it. Because it hurts to have an inchoate piece of work on hand, my natural response has been to try to bring it to completion as quickly as possible. Thus, I prove to myself that I can indeed finish it, and I'm able to get a quick sense of the value of the piece. But by rushing some of my writing, I've produced in it a kind of thinness, or an unrealized quality. So I've had to work hard at developing some methods for dealing with the Urge Toward Premature Completion (UTPC).

For me, the "soft copy" state of a piece of writing offered by word-processing is an ideal antidote to UTPC. Contrary to the computer-paranoiac conventional wisdom of immediately printing up a "hard copy" of a day's work, I find that keeping my writing *off the page* has a benefit: when it exists on the screen but not yet on paper, my project always seems to me more speculative, something I'm just trying out. I feel much more willing to risk tentatively conceived thoughts, word-choices, metaphors, character-actions; if these from-the-hip decisions turn out to be "wrong," then they can simply be zapped from the screen. Once deleted, no evidence of these wrong decisions is left. So my natural anxiety about making a fool out of myself is lowered; I feel free to take a chance on anything that occurs to me.

As all we computer-addicts know, one of the great benefits of word-processing is that we're not penalized for our revisions with the hard labor of retyping. This license to make changes is especially valid while a document is in soft copy. Improvements don't even result in wasted ink and paper. So when I go over what I wrote yesterday, I've had time to think about what I might have set forth only tentatively, time to refine it conceptually as well as in its smallest details. And now that I've got a day's worth of distance from the writing, I can see it freshly. (Which phenomena suggest that non-writing time contributes a great deal to actual writing time.) With my refreshed perspective, I do not hesitate to make any change large or small. The piece is immensely changeable, as flexible as my mental processes will allow it to be.

After some five years of getting used to working with soft copy, revising yesterday's writing on the computer screen has become as natural for me as merely reading it over. So this is my primary tactic against UTPC—to keep a writing-project in soft copy all the way through its first draft. Of some benefit also is reading and editing the entire document at least once from start to finish before I ever commit myself to "hard copy" by printing it up.

But once the copy has been printed, then UTPC gains the advantage over us computer-addicts: my laser-printed first draft can look terrific, especially if I've done a great deal of revising before it ever hits the page. It's too easy for me to adore my project when it comes off the printer that first time. I've had to train myself to resist such literary puppy love.

My method for dealing with this phase of UTPC is to fall back to the old ways, the old tools: I sit down with a red pen to annotate the manuscript as thoroughly as I possibly can. I try to be excessive with the red pen. I try to convert that polished-looking document into a real mess.

Since it's easy to reproduce word-processed manuscripts, I also hand out copies of my work-in-progress to my writing friends and ask them to exercise their red pens freely. I collect these messed-up manuscripts, take them back to my desk and address each annotation with the document on the screen in front of me. Sometimes I ignore a critical observation or don't take a suggestion offered by one of my friends, but I do sit there and think about it with the possibility of making a change immediately available to me.

The further along I follow this process of finishing a piece of writing, the less mystery there is to it. At the very end, when I'm down to changing a word here and a comma there, what began as merely an idea and somewhere along the line (if the piece is any good) became mystery has now returned to pure method—to my trying to make the final draft of the manuscript as scrupulously "correct" as possible. This part is as mechanical and easy as beginning in the upper left hand corner. Finally, I press three keys, and my computer directs the printer to produce this thing I've written that is mysteriously so much better than anything I could possibly have written.

10 COMPOSING POETRY ON A COMPUTER:
Word-Processing and the Poetic Line

Of all kinds of writers, the most computer-resistant have been poets. In *Harper's*, Wendell Berry says he won't use a computer because of its being part of an energy-wasting technology. In *The New York Times Book Review,* Louis Simpson says he won't use a computer because it would undermine his faith in the permanence of the lines he composes. A poet friend of mine gets a call from his editor in response to a letter my friend wrote him in which he mentioned that he had recently purchased a computer; the editor blurts, "John, you're not going to write your poems on that thing, are you?" Even some computer-devotees among my poetry-writing acquaintances won't compose their first drafts of poems on the computer; for revision they'll bring the poem to word-processing only after they've drafted it in handwriting.

More than in any other kind of writing, the forces of magic—or of the muse—are believed to operate in the composition of poetry. Among poets that magic is commonly believed to be threatened by the use of the computer in the composition process.

I'm certain I'm not the only one, but I'd bet I'm among a small minority of poets who believe that the poetic muse finds the computer hospitable. There are mornings when I believe that she frolics to her heart's content among the microchips inside that beige colored box beneath my computer screen. I am certain that word-processing has given me my best poems.

To be specific, my word-processing program has liberated my sense of possibility in the poetic line. Its division of language into discrete lines is what distinguishes poetry from prose. The essence of poetry—the music, the play, the power of it—resides in the poetic line. In traditional rhymed and metered poetry, line breaks are determined by formal considerations: e.g., a line of blank verse will be ten syllables long with an iambic accentual pattern—five *ta-dum's*, as I tell my beginning creative writing classes. In free verse, the poet determines where the line breaks, according to personal inclinations and an individual's sense of poetic form. The poet has been granted license to do as he or she pleases with respect to the basic poetic instrument, the poetic line. Word-processing facilitates experimenting with the poetic line so that the poet can explore those personal inclinations. Put simply, word-processing makes it easier for a poet to try out different line breaks and decide what to do in a given poetic line.

Here are selections from a couple of weeks' worth of revisions of a section of a poem of mine, arranged from earliest to most recent.

1.   A bird
        flashes diagonally up
        and across the streaked glass,
        crow or hawk, there and gone so fast
        my mind can hardly register it.

2.   A bird
        flashes diagonally up
        and across the streaked glass
        big shadow there and gone so fast
        my mind can hardly register it...

3.   A bird
        flashes diagonally up
        and across the streaked glass
        winged shadow there and gone so fast
        it barely catches my eye, my mind
        drifting from my work,

4.   A bird
        flashes diagonally up
        and across the streaked glass,
        winged shadow there and gone almost
        too fast for my mind to register
        what I think I've seen.

5.   A bird
        flashes diagonally up
        across the wet-streaked glass
        winged shadow there and gone almost
        too fast for my mind to register
        what I might have seen,

6.   A bird
        flashes diagonally up
        across the wet-streaked glass,
        winged shadow there and gone so fast
        I barely see it,

These selections represent about a third of the number of hard copy versions of this section of the poem and about a twentieth of the number of soft copy versions of it. I mean for this poem to have the appearance of being in free verse, but in my composition process, strictly for my own benefit, I've imposed a discipline of an eight-syllable line as a means of clarifying and condensing my thought and my language.

Along with the discipline of line length goes the general discipline I'd impose on any poem, that of trying to "engineer" weak words away from line endings and strong words out to the ends of the lines. Thus *bird, up, glass,* and *fast* are words that, because of the poetic line, automatically benefit from a little highlighting in my reader's mind. In a few early soft copy versions of the poem, *flashes* was a word that I'd engineered out to a line ending, but I let it go down as a line beginning because for a while the poem was titled "Flash," and therefore the word didn't need any extra emphasis—in fact I need my poetic line to de-emphasize the word to avoid too heavy-handedly presenting my theme of temporality. Though the poem's title was later changed, I'd used the word *flashing* further along in the text, and so I still needed to de-emphasize the word. Thus one of the hundreds of small changes I made in this poem was from this:

A bird flashes

diagonally up across...

to this:

A bird

flashes diagonally up...

The particular word-processing skill I've developed which has liberated my sense of the poetic line is that of manipulating my cursor, my backspace key, and my "enter" (or "return") key, so as to be able very quickly to try out different combinations of lines. By placing my cursor under the first letter of the first word of a line and backspacing twice, I add that line to the one above it:

in thin rain that's chilling us both,

shivering us hard these minutes

instantly becomes

in thin rain that's chilling us both, shivering us hard

these minutes.

Then, by placing my cursor at the place where I want to try breaking the line and tapping the "enter" key, I can have a look at a new arrangement:

> in thin rain that's chilling us both, shivering
> us hard these minutes

or

> in thin rain that's chilling
> us both, shivering us hard
> these minutes.

The changes in the lines above are strictly changes in the line breaks. But in the process of tinkering with the line breaks, a poet sees new possibilities of phrasing and word choice. Thus compare the final version of the ending of this poem:

> as a crow lights,
> bobbing a limb of my neighbor's spruce,
> or lifts and flies through fifty miles
> of rain before it comes to rest

with this earlier version:

> as a crow
> sometimes lights in the neighbor's spruce,
> sometimes flies through
> a hundred miles
> of rain before it comes to rest.

The earlier version repeats the inconsequential word *sometimes*, doesn't give the line ending emphasis to the consequential word *lights*, doesn't provide the visually appealing bobbing branch, and exaggerates the amount of flying through rain that a crow might accomplish. These differences are substantial, but they evolved out of a concern for the poetic line. The improvements I brought about are a direct result of my easily being able to manipulate my lines and to see on the screen (in soft copy) and on the page (in hard copy) what my options were.

In many ways the manipulative skills I'm describing here are a sort of advanced form of typing, but they are typing skills that became available only with word-processing. If I composed on a typewriter or even with a pencil and a pad of paper, I would have to "pay for" the privilege of checking out my options with a considerable amount of uncreative labor: each version of a line that I wished to see would mean retyping, or re(hand)writing the line again. Such labor is, unavoidably, an inhibiting factor in the writing process: because checking out each option would penalize me with a given amount of labor, I wouldn't check them all out. My mind would hesitate: I simply wouldn't think of something—e.g., the bobbing limb—because the way to reach a new possibility would be blocked by the obstacle of necessary labor. In word-processing, it's not only easy to check out the options, it even becomes a form of play—a peculiarly poetic form of play. Nowadays I'm likely to refine my poem much more thoroughly than I might have if I'd composed it on a typewriter.

Paradoxically enough, though I've described a method of facilitating the creative process, I haven't said that word-processing makes writing poetry any easier. The fact is that opening up these possibilities of exploring the poetic line actually increases the difficulty of writing poetry. But any true poet could only welcome such increased difficulty since it opens up the way for a more accomplished poetry. Each additional option must be pursued; the thoughts and feelings that inevitably accompany these new options must also be followed out to their conclusions. Nowadays, I find that I produce about twice as many hard copies of a poem as I did back in the prehistoric seven years ago when I composed my poems on a typewriter. Because word-processing has facilitated my ability to envision possibilities of the poetic line, the actual project of composing and finishing a poem has become much more challenging and demanding. But word-processing has also increased my pleasure in composition and offered me a higher reward in the form of poems of greater depth, complexity, and force. My poems take me further than they ever did before. I'm delighted to confess that I have no choice but to go along with them.

APPENDIX:

Study

This morning rain on my skylight
marbles the blue-gray sky and blurs
the maple's branches suffering
the wind from the northeast.
                              A bird
flashes diagonally up
across the wet-streaked glass,
winged shadow there and gone so fast
I barely see it,
                  then standing
at my grandmother's grave, I feel
my mother lean against me, wind
and cold rain slapping our faces
for letting Gran die by herself
in a hateful room;
                    and driving
through mountains in a slick-tired VW
with one headlight gone, I'm swabbing
fog off the windshield while rain turns
to snow;
            dark is coming, and I

am saying goodbye to Linda
Butler on Dundalk Avenue
in thin rain that's chilling us both,
shivering us hard these minutes
that are the last we ever spend
together;
             a boy on a porch
smells rain coming across the fields
and sees his young father running
toward him with drops splattering
his shirt;
             a child out in the yard
hears his aunt laugh as he strips off
clothes in a thunderstorm—
                              quick light
flashing down corridors darkened
by all these years!—
                       as a crow lights,
bobbing a limb of my neighbor's spruce,
or lifts and flies through fifty miles
of rain before it comes to rest.

11 TAKING WHAT YOU NEED, GIVING WHAT YOU CAN:
The Writer as Student and Teacher

The kind of writer and the kind of teacher of writing I am these days is powerfully informed by my experience as a student of writing. As an undergraduate I had four semesters of creative writing, and I completed the work for two different graduate writing programs. Altogether I studied under eleven different writing teachers. If ever there was a product of the American Creative Writing Industry, I am it. And yet in the composition of this essay, I have come to realize that I came to my education equipped with an essential quality, without which I never would have become any kind of writer at all: I was able to take what I needed from every teacher and every class, and I was able to disregard what I didn't need or what might have harmed me. I'm not sure what to name this quality—survival aptitude, perhaps—but it seems to me necessary for anyone who aspires to make a writing life for him- or herself. It seems to me the one quality that perhaps you are born with or born without. If you have it—if you can take what you need from your experience to nourish your writing—then you can learn to write, and the classroom will be of enormous benefit to you. If you don't have it, then no amount of writing education will make you a writer.

So I know that writing can be taught, but I also know that only a small number of people can learn to be writers. In my writing classes, I encounter many students who have more talent, more writerly resources (e.g., intelligence, language aptitude, literary instinct) than I have ever had, but who do not become writers. I also encounter a few students whose talents and resources are modest but who nevertheless become writers. In the past, I have been frustrated by such unlikely results of my classes. Nowadays I am comforted by that unpredictable element of teaching writing.

In composing this essay and discussing it with my writer friends, I've come to see that just as a real writer takes what he or she needs from a teacher, so, too, does a writing teacher give what he or she can. It is not my duty to tailor my teaching to each individual student; it is not my duty to attempt to make writers of my students. It is my duty to be a certain kind of teacher, to try to be consistent in the values that I try to convey to my students, and to let them use me as they will—as I used my teachers.

My relationship with writing and with literature is a practical one. I was years coming to understand this relationship, and in the process, I flunked out of the University of Virginia as an English Major. In 1962 and '63, I knew that I was powerfully affected by many of the novels, stories, and poems I was reading for my classes, but I couldn't get the hang of writing papers, saying the right things in class, or *thinking about literature* in the way that apparently my professors thought about it. Not only that, some of the lectures and discussions from those classes seemed to me deeply wrong but in a way that I couldn't even approach articulating.

I remember three different occasions of English major stall-out—trying to write papers on Salinger's *Nine Stories*, Conrad's *Nostromo*, and Melville's *Moby Dick*. These were books I deeply loved. I wasn't able to make myself write those papers because (I later understood) I couldn't connect what I felt about the books with the way—the conventional way—I thought the papers had to be written. This wasn't really the fault of my literature professors; if I had been able to think of an alternative and personally meaningful way for me to write the papers, my instructors most likely would have accommodated me, perhaps even rewarded me for being innovative. But at the age of 20, I didn't have enough gumption to invent my own alternative methods.

What's the difference between academic and practical approaches to narrative literature? Thematic concerns, symbolism, literary history, and matters of influence were, in those days, the stuff of the academic approach to literature. A practical-minded reader would be drawn to such elements as characterization, situation, point of view, structure, setting, pacing, symmetry, diction, syntax, and sentence length. An academic teacher is—or was in those days—interested in the ultimate value of a literary work and its connection to other literary works; a writing teacher is interested in how a work works and does not work.

I'm still reacting to those academically-inclined professors. Workshop is the word that I put forth in opposition to whatever I see as academic. I'm a committed workshop teacher. I constantly try to show my students the value of a practical approach, not only to manuscripts that pass through our classrooms, but also to works of literature. I want the writing workshop to be a place where it is all right to love *The Sound and the Fury* for entirely different reasons than those that make it attractive to professors and A-plus students of Modern American Literature.

As part of the practical approach to literature, I want my students to see that most aspects of a literary work are down-to-earth matters that are perfectly understandable to a moderately intelligent reader using common sense. Throughout my high school and undergraduate education I encountered teachers who saw literature as apprehensible by only an elite few. This literature-as-a-high-mystery approach elevates the teacher who espouses it at the same time it excuses that teacher from having to be rigorous-minded in actually thinking about the work itself. This is a centuries-old literary-pedagogical tradition, but I tend to be personally irked about it. The message of that kind of teaching is that there is such an immense distance between literature and the student that the idea of any but the most gifted student's having literary aspirations is absurd. I now feel that such teaching conspired to deny me and others like me our rightful literary heritage. So one of my basic aims in the classroom is to try to return that heritage to practical-minded students.

Some of the practical aspects of writing I wish to reflect in my teaching are as follows:

Writing is a natural act. You don't have to be somebody else to write well. Because they've been taught that literature is so far "above" them, many of my students feel that they must spout philosophical profundities, espouse noble sentiments, and compose archaically poetical phrases. In short, many of my students see the act of trying to make literature as one that by definition requires them to be other than themselves. And this illusion is not easily shattered. My project for a semester of beginning poetry- and fiction-writing may be generally described as trying to coax a room full of 20-year-olds to try to be—or to discover—themselves in their writing.

Reading is also a natural act for a writer. Reading is writing's nourishment. Like anyone else, a writer reads for pleasure and instruction, but there is another level at which writers read: ruthlessly and automatically, they consume the writing technology of what they read. Writers learn the craft of writing by reading the work of other writers. I don't think writers of integrity steal from other writers in any direct way, but I do think they incorporate other writers' technology into their own systems. No writer of integrity would say to himself, "Ah, yes, Salinger switches from the first-person to the third-person point of view here in the middle of "For Esmé with Love and Squalor," and I am going to write a story utilizing this very successful device." At the same time, I think that any serious writer would not read "For Esmé with Love and Squalor" without being struck by that change in point of view, without thinking about it, and without incorporating observations and conclusions about that device into his or her own writing technology. Imitating the device itself would be the crudest articulation of influence. But the reading writer's future point-of-view decisions are likely to be informed by the Salinger story.

Within their individual sensibilities—the true source of originality—writers carry around what they've learned from other writers. Within that part of me that is peculiar to David Huddle also reside William Faulkner, Ernest Hemingway, Peter Taylor, Eudora Welty, Flannery O'Connor, Raymond Carver, John Cheever, J.D. Salinger, Richard Yates, George P. Elliott, Hannah Green, and two or three hundred other writers. I am honored to have them as my guests.

My teaching reflects my experience of having my writing nourished by my reading. I use anthologies in class, read stories and poems aloud in class and discuss them with my writing students. To help students with specific problems or issues in their writing, I often refer them to such-and-such a story, poem, book, or writer, and I lend my books to students who seem to me serious and likely to return the books.

I wish all of my discussions of writing to be informed by my reading, and I wish to demonstrate to students that I carry out my writing life in the company of other writers carrying out their writing lives. I wish to demonstrate to students that I am a writer primarily because I love other writers' stories, novels, poems, and essays. Occasionally I'll put it bluntly to a student: if you don't love reading short stories, then you have no business trying to write them.

Criticism—or responding verbally to manuscripts—is a natural act. In this case, I have a two-front war to wage with my students: there are those who wish to make pronouncements about the worksheets that we discuss (e.g., "This story fails because its author stereotypes the main characters") and there are those who feel that they are not trained critics and therefore they have no business criticizing anyone's work and furthermore an author's story is the way it is because that's how the author wanted it to be and who are they to take issue with the author's intentions?

One tactic I exercise here is to ascribe esthetic will to literary works; I suggest that stories yearn toward a state of perfection, that it is up to an author to give a story what *it* wants or needs, and that it is up to a critic to help the author discern a story's desires. This is not nearly as much of a fairy tale as it sounds in this fast version; my own experience of writing has been one of developing sensitivity to the signals my work is giving me as I compose it. I tell my students that when I first began writing, I always had a plan and I stuck to it as strictly as possible, trying to ignore the distracting ideas that came to me in the composing process; I tell them that I still begin with a plan, but that nowadays I try to accept most of the ideas that come to me in the composing process. I tell them that such ideas are, in my opinion, true inspiration, and that I have found the inspiration that comes this way, from within the work, to be much more reliable and useful than the other kind, the kind that comes when you're taking a walk in the woods, watching a sunset, or listening to your favorite music.

I also employ "pretend-devices" designed to free up a critic to express opinions that are withheld because of social inhibition. The easiest one is to ask, "Sarah, if this story were yours, what would be the first thing you'd try to change in it?" A student who would never dream of saying, "I think you ought to develop the male character," would think it perfectly all right to say, "If this were my story, I'd try to develop the male character a little more." A similar "pretend device" of mine goes this way, "Let's say this is your story, and you sent it to *The New Yorker* and they sent it back to you saying, 'We loved this story, but we think it needs to be cut by about a page and a half.' Where would you do the cutting, Sarah?" In this case, Sarah might not wish to suggest cutting the story even while pretending she wrote it, but pretending that she wrote it and that *The New Yorker* wants her to cut it will allow her to see and to say exactly where the story should be edited.

Receiving criticism may not be a natural act, but it is a valuable skill, very much worth developing. A crucial introduction to this development can be the standard workshop practice of requiring an author to be silent during the discussion of his or her work. A workshop where an author can't keep quiet but feels compelled to defend and explain the work under discussion is a counterproductive experience for both the author and the people who are trying to offer helpful criticism.

Nowadays, before a class's first workshop session, I try to set forth the ground rules in such a way as to designate the author's place in the discussion as one of privilege. I'll try to say something like, "Knowing that you will have the last say in the discussion, you authors may sit back and listen from a vantage point of serene detachment." I recommend that the author try to take notes because 1) taking notes helps you to keep your mouth shut and 2) notes help you remember useful remarks you might forget under the influence of the emotional state authors usually find themselves in when their work is discussed. I remind the class that workshop discussions are solely for the benefit of the author; they do not take place so that critics can show off for each other, and they do not take place so that an author can explain the work to its readers. Workshops take place so that readers can communicate to an author how his or her work has affected them and what possibilities they see within the work. I remind authors that they are not required to accept any of the criticism they are offered, but I suggest that they not be hasty in rejecting it. A suggestion that seems insulting during and immediately after the discussion may next week be the key to a brilliant revision. Ideally, over the course of days and weeks, authors will consider the discussion of their work and will make changes at their leisure.

It is easy for a writing teacher, who might have participated in several thousand workshop sessions, to forget what a traumatic experience it can be for a student who has never, or has seldom, had the experience of having a story or poem publicly discussed. When I was a graduate student at Columbia, I was often a brutal critic of my fellow students' work; I felt personally insulted by writing I thought not to be good, I wasn't above showing off for my instructors and the other students I respected, and I figured I owed it to weak writers to discourage them from pursuing an activity that was sure to bring them disappointment. As a teacher, over the years, I have encouraged myself to try to be kinder and more positive in my criticism, especially in what I express in the public forum of the workshop. It is one thing to write a student a note about a manuscript that conveys the suggestion that a higher quality of work is in order; it is quite another to humiliate a student in a class. I try to monitor the schedule of presentations so that a student has a chance to present his or her best story to the workshop. And if something is dreadfully wrong with a story that is presented, rather than harping on the wrongness of it, I try to persuade participants to suggest various ways of solving the problem.

In my last ten years of teaching, I have learned the value of responding in writing to student manuscripts: In order to write a response to a manuscript I have to think harder about it than I would if I were speaking aloud about it in class or in a conference with the student; writing clarifies my thinking and demands that I try to make my thinking useful for the student-author. From the student's view, it helps to have a written response so that faulty memory doesn't erase or alter the instructor's observations; the tangibility of a written response can encourage a higher quality of revision. It also helps to have a written response from the instructor before a story goes before a workshop, so that a student can have some idea of how the discussion might proceed.

Out of writing responses to hundreds of manuscripts, I have developed a technique that I call "diplomatic syntax." Here's a crude example: would you rather someone said to you, "You have beautiful eyes, but you have bad breath," or "You have bad breath, but you have beautiful eyes"? The literal message of the sentence is that you have these two qualities, beautiful eyes and bad breath, but the syntax of the first example makes the bad breath more important than the beautiful eyes whereas the opposite is the case in the second example. So most of us would probably prefer to hear, "You have bad breath, but you have beautiful eyes." Getting the news that way would probably send us to brush our teeth while studying our eyes in the bathroom mirror. Getting it the other way might send us to our rooms to cry or pout.

Here's how diplomatic syntax is used in written responses to student writing. Let's say I'm trying to respond to a story that has the following qualities:

A. The action is exaggerated.

B. The characters are stereotypes.

C. The writing is cliché-riddled.

D. There is only one believable scene in the whole story.

Let's say that this is a student's first short story, and in spite of the low quality of the work, I want to be as encouraging as possible. To convey my sense of the relative importance of the story's problems, I might begin my note to the student this way:

> Although you have a strong scene on page 6, you have at least three major problems to deal with here: the action is so exaggerated that a reader can't take it seriously, your characters are such stereotypes that a reader knows their lines before they say them, and you've used so many clichés that reading your prose is like eating last week's corn muffins.

As a teacher and as a writer constantly engaged in the

struggle to write well, I know it's sometimes hard to resist composing that kind of note because it conveys to the student just how far away his or her work is from writing of an acceptable quality. But as a student, if I get a note like that about a story I've worked pretty hard on, my discouragement is likely to obliterate any illumination I might receive from it. So here's how a teacher might convey the same criticism but couched (an appropriate verb here) in diplomatic syntax:

> Although you need to work on making the story's action more credible, developing and individualizing your characters, and freshening up your prose, you've nevertheless written a terrific scene on page 6 that demonstrates the principles you need to apply to the story's other scenes. When that girl walks out of that bar and says, "I won't be coming back to this place any more," that is an utterly believable scene, and that line of dialogue you've given her is exactly the kind of thing you need to have her saying elsewhere.

One might argue that diplomatic syntax is nothing more than sugar-coating the truth. I would counter by pointing out that a professional writer and teacher of writing has such highly developed critical faculties that encountering something wrong in a manuscript causes a mental red light to start blinking madly and a relentless inner voice to begin chanting, "Fix it! Fix it! Fix it!" But this extreme response needs to be translated into terms useful to a beginning writer. What the apprentice has done well quite often can be the foundation upon which to build a sense of critical values. If an apprentice can see that he or she has written one good scene, there is at least a chance that the difference between that scene and the unsuccessful scenes will become evident, and personal critical values can begin to be formed.

Beginning writers are not the only ones with tender feelings, though. Every semester, in my beginning poetry-and fiction-writing classes, I read one of my own stories and some of my own poems to my students. This is not a pedagogical activity for the thin-skinned. In a workshop of fifteen or sixteen people, there will always be at least one who can ask a devastating question. ("Why did that girl walk out of that bar that way?") Nowadays I pride myself on not being defensive in class, on listening carefully, and on making it clear that I will consider anything and everything that is said to me about my work. This is not just acting on my part; I have benefited a great deal from criticism I have received from my writing classes. But that doesn't mean that I don't often walk out of such classes with my soul bleeding. ("Didn't they understand that she walked out of the bar because of the song playing on the jukebox?")

But I'm a better writer for having submitted my writing to the workshop for scrutiny, and I hope my workshops are more nourishing communities as a result of my having brought my work into them. An important lesson I took from George Garrett, my mentor at Hollins College in 1968-69, was the value of a writer-teacher's companionship. That Garrett treated me like a writer helped me begin thinking of myself as a writer. At the time he was treating me so generously, I questioned his judgment and diminished the amount of esteem I accorded to him. We're all familiar with that dynamic: "If he thinks I'm a writer, then he can't be all that great a writer himself." Nowadays I understand what a noble thing it is that George has done over the years for his many hundreds of writing students: he has extended himself toward us in such an absolutely democratic way as to prevent the kind of idolization that many other writing teachers encourage. By treating us as writers, he helped us become writers. Garrett's manner toward his students requires them to see him as a regular guy trying as best he can to get some good writing done. There could certainly be no more useful an example for an apprentice writer.

I've been lucky to have had a number of writing teachers whose treatment of me as a fellow-artist has helped me carry out my work. The first story-writing class I took was at the University of Virginia in 1963 from a formidable non-writer, Professor John Coleman, a brittle-witted, quick-tongued guy whose practice it was to read the students' stories aloud in class and to correct and ridicule them as he read them. In some cases, he had the student read his own story aloud—by coming to the front and standing before the class—but he continued to interrupt with corrections and comments in the course of the reading.

There were two or three of us that he favored, and I was lucky in that I received Coleman's mercy, but his general technique for that class was to set us students against each other in seeking his approval. Virginia was an all-male school then, and the atmosphere of that classroom had a kind of locker-room ruthlessness about it. We laughed at our classmates as they were subjected to Coleman's humiliations; his teaching conspired to make us admire him and to despise each other.

My next writing teacher was James Kraft, a young man who'd just received his doctorate from Virginia, a very energetic and hospitable teacher. Kraft wasn't a published writer, but he had been working on a novel for a while, and he wasn't cruel. I came to this class, in the summer of 1967, straight out of the army's 25th Military Intelligence Detachment stationed in Cu Chi, Vietnam, and of course what I was writing then were stories about military experience. Between being discharged from the army in Oakland, California, and coming to Charlottesville, I'd spent a week with my parents in Louisville, Kentucky, sunbathing by their apartment complex swimming pool, trying to impress the lifeguard, a pretty high school girl named Nancy. In my heroic efforts, I'd dived into water that was too shallow and had skinned my nose rather dramatically. So I showed up in Jim Kraft's class as this Vietnam Vet looking dark-skinned and recently wounded, as if I'd just stepped out of the jungle with a string of Vietcong ears attached to my belt. Kraft and the other students treated me with a rather horrified respect, and whatever I might have written, they were not likely to criticize it harshly. I wasn't writing stories with much authenticity, but Kraft addressed my work with a seriousness that always surprised me. I remember that the one nonmilitary story I wrote had a character in it named Leviticus—simply because I liked the sound of that name—and preparing for class the night before that story came up for discussion, Kraft read the entire book of Leviticus, trying to understand my Biblical allusion. If he was irked when I told him that I had no reason other than the sound of it for using that name, he didn't let on. From him I learned as a writer not to be careless in my choices and as a would-be teacher that taking a student's writing seriously encourages the student to take it seriously, too.

Peter Taylor was my next writing teacher, for his first and my last two semesters at the University of Virginia. Though I later came to revere him, in 1967 Taylor was no one I'd ever heard of. He had a humble, shambling air about him that did not encourage veneration. In class his manner was without authority. He brought in books and read aloud from them, mostly Chekhov, though I also heard him read Faulkner's "That Evening Sun," and Caroline Gordon's "Old Red," and a fair portion of Katherine Ann Porter's "Old Mortality." He spoke about characters and scenes the way you'd talk about things that happened in your family or among your friends. This was in a graduate-level class—he had been kind enough to let me enroll in it—and for about the first month and a half, he read to us in class and talked with us in this unsettlingly ordinary way about what he'd read. I had handed in a couple of stories, and I was impatient to have them discussed in class, and I knew that several other students were even more disturbed than I was at Taylor's unproductive use of our class time.

Taylor held conferences with some of us about stories. He had an office in a little dimly-lit, musty-smelling house on the other side of Jefferson Park Avenue from Cabell Hall, and over there, too, he seemed to me to lack the exotic aura I expected a real writer to have. It was sort of like going into your uncle's law office and talking about your plans to attend law school. Taylor did not go over your manuscript sentence by sentence. Rather, he spoke in general terms about disappointingly non-literary issues of the story and about fiction-writing in general. A couple of things I remember his telling me were that it was awfully hard finding what you wanted to write about and that he had been grateful to see that his subject matter was family. He also told me once of his father's being mad at him about a story he wrote which had a character in it very much like a family aunt; his father had met him at the airport shortly after the story's publication and told him that if Taylor had been around when the father read it, the father would have hit him. He told me that he sometimes left blanks in his stories when he couldn't think of the right word or the right sentence; he said that he liked going over and over his stories because it gave them a kind of "gnarled" quality.

Taylor requested a conference with me to talk about one of my stories that I'd been especially eager to have discussed in class. Its denouement came in a scene where a man and a woman are engaged in sex in the female-superior position on a kitchen table when the woman's husband comes in and murders her with a shotgun. Now that I remember it, it seems to me that Taylor took me into a small room behind his office for our conference, and it became evident to me that talking about this story embarrassed him a great deal, but he gave me to understand it was a lesser embarrassment than trying to lead a discussion of it in class would have been. One of the things he said then was that he personally had nothing against a dirty story—he claimed to have written a few of them himself—but that he didn't think a person who might not wish to read such a story ought to have one inflicted on him- or herself in a workshop. If that session sticks in my mind, it also sticks in Peter's. From then on, over the years, whenever anyone reported back to me that they'd seen Peter Taylor and mentioned my name to him, they'd say he shook his head over the kind of stories I was writing in those days. So far as I know, Peter still thinks of me as a quasi-pornographer.

When Peter finally did get around to discussing our stories in class, he took it upon himself to read them aloud to us. He said that he thought it would be useful for us to hear our stories read in another voice and to hear all of them read in the same voice. Well, he was right about that, you could hear things about your story when he read it that wouldn't have been evident otherwise. If he had trouble with a sentence, you knew it needed some reworking; if he read a passage as if he savored it, you knew you'd done something right. Again, his actual talk about our stories was so ordinary and commonsensical that it frustrated me and frustrated most of us. We'd jump in with negative observations whenever possible, and Peter let us have our say, but most often he was in the position of defending a story against the criticism of a majority of the class. At the time, this way of running a workshop seemed to me all wrong and further evidence that Peter Taylor wasn't much of a writer and wasn't really suited to be a writing teacher.

In spite of his reservations over my subject matter, Peter Taylor unobtrusively brought about a personal relationship with me that I think in some part was calculated to enable me to know him, to know something about his life as a writer.

My regard for Peter Taylor's work and his teaching has increased over the years, and I now see that even at the time I was in his classes, I was learning more than I thought I was. For one thing, it was the first genuine workshop I'd attended. We students were encouraged to form bonds with each other, even if some of the bonding came out of our impatience with Peter. John Coleman and Jim Kraft had been good writing teachers for me, but their's had been writing *classes*—in that the channels of energy went from student to professor and back from professor to student—not *workshops*—in which the class is a community of writers working with each other under the leadership of a senior writer.

After Peter Taylor at Virginia and George Garrett at Hollins, I entered Columbia University's MFA Program where my first teacher was Richard Elman, a quintessential New York City writer. I'd done a good deal of writing the summer before I moved to New York, and so I brought in about 125 pages of new work to show my new writing teacher. A few days later, Elman held a conference with me in which he told me very bluntly that if I was going to write like that, he would have no interest in me throughout my time at Columbia. This was devastating for me, because at considerable sacrifice and expense, my wife and I had moved to the city so that I could attend Columbia, and now Columbia, in the voice of Richard Elman, was telling me before I even got started that I was a failure. In my opinion that was a reckless thing for a teacher to do to a student. Elman's point, as I now understand it, was that I was trying to rely more on craft than on heart, and somewhere along the line I did need to have that news delivered to me. I spent a month or so feeling lousy about it, but then I started writing my way out of my doldrums. I felt like I had survived an assault on my writing life, and I felt stronger for having done so. So even though I would probably not be so blunt as Elman was, I give him credit for having done something for me that a writing teacher can sometimes do for a student—get him back on the right track.

Hannah Green was my second writing teacher at Columbia. Compared with Richard Elman, Hannah was an angel of positive reinforcement and a very low-profiled presence in the workshop.

Among her rare qualities was her capacity to be affected by what she heard or read in class. She responded very emotionally to workshop work, and she was unembarrassed about her responses, valuable behavior for me to witness, since I had schooled myself in the Faulkner-Hemingway ethic of holding back emotion as both a personal and a literary code. One particular memory of Hannah that I hold very close is of sitting beside her during Tillie Olsen's visit to our class and Tillie's reading of "Hey Sailor, What Ship?" The story is about the pain of an alcoholic's destruction witnessed by people who have loved and respected him, and while I sat listening to it, I found my eyes focused on Hannah's wrist, which at some time in her life had been broken and had healed at a slightly crooked angle. I was also aware of some small sounds Hannah made as we listened to the story together, quiet Oh's and Um's that registered the story's hurt. I of course didn't weep because of the story, but Hannah did, openly and unashamedly. In some part I feel that Hannah Green legitimized my emotional involvement in my reading and in my teaching, and she reinforced the value I'd already taken from Taylor and Garrett, that a writer's company was at least as valuable as his or her classroom teaching.

The one truly bad writing teacher I have ever had was Anthony Burgess, who was working for both Columbia and Princeton in the same term and was living in New Jersey. Burgess would take no student manuscript home with him to read and would hold no office hours with any student. A few aggressive ones gave him rides to and from the airport in order to have some personal contact with him. He was always late for his classes, and he seemed to blame us for it; once he came in almost an hour late and shouted at us who had sat around the seminar table waiting for him, "I don't know what you people want from me!" He left early whenever he could get by with it. During class time, he went around the seminar table, holding mini-conferences with students, looking at a page of their work, skimming down that page until he found a word choice that he wished to discuss. He held forth for a while on a particular word, and then he moved on to the next student. After three weeks of Burgess, I managed to transfer out of his class and back to Richard Elman's; Elman might have been a reckless teacher, but at least he took his teaching duties seriously. Nevertheless, I learned about teaching from Burgess the way you can learn about writing by reading a really lousy book.

Lore Segal was my writing teacher for my final semester at Columbia. This was during a time when Lore was recovering from the loss of her husband David to a heart attack. She wasn't sleeping very well that spring, and she spent her hours of insomnia annotating the thesis manuscripts of those of her students who were graduating. Lore made it clear that she liked my stories, but the work she did on them with her editing pencil was rigorous and intimidating. From her, I learned a view of teaching writing that connects liking somebody's work with giving it the most painstaking scrutiny. For me, this continues to be a necessary principle since my natural lazy inclination is to think that if I like something, it probably doesn't need much editorial attention from me. I'm still a pretty lazy manuscript annotator, but I do have Lore's good example firmly planted in my brain.

This has been a roundabout way of demonstrating that my own teachers' primary gifts to me were not the exotic secrets of writing but were in fact the ordinary methods of living a writing life and making human connections with other writers. One of the things I have had most trouble grasping is the letting-go part of the connections between writer-friends. For years I wrote letters to Peter Taylor dutifully reporting to him my professional progress. Once or twice I got a politely phrased postcard from him, but never a letter. On the teacher side of things, I'm still corresponding with so many of my old students that letter-writing often gets in the way of my own writing.

A writing workshop is, in its ideal sense, a community of writers trying to help each other accomplish their best writing. Its first level of value is in its being a community, a gathering of people whose company nourishes each person's writing life. What a workshop is not is a committee that repairs faulty manuscripts. Most of the time manuscripts can be improved through sensitive revision in response to workshop discussion. But the process is not a mechanical one in which critics tell the author what is wrong with a story and how to fix it, and the author goes home and does what the workshop told him to do. The dynamic of a workshop is oblique, indirect, subtle, and occasionally perverse. Listening to workshop discussion of one story may lead an author to a realization of how to write another, much more urgently felt story. Listening to workshop discussion of a story's ending may bring the author to a solution of a problem with the story's beginning, of which only the author is aware. I believe that workshops can be immensely useful but that they are only rarely useful in obvious and logical ways. I also believe that their usefulness is strongly determined by the members' level of commitment to their community. When writers care enough about the work of other writers to give it their time and attention, everybody's work is nourished.

Some of the most valuable things I have been taught as a writer are intangibles that come out of my having carried on my work in the company of other writers carrying on their work. These are values that I hope to pass on to my students, both in and out of workshops, through example, through mental telepathy, through having these values inform everything I say about writing. These are elements of a writers' code, and though I can't articulate them all, I can nevertheless give you an idea of what I'm talking about:

◆ The one relationship that counts is the one between you and your writing. If you feel good about what you're working on, then you're in good shape, and if you don't feel good about it, then you need to figure out what to change so that you do feel good about it. What you're working on right now is what matters, not what you have written and not what you're going to write.

◆ Writing is writing's reward. The best part of story-writing is to be working on a story in which you are wholeheartedly and wholemindedly engaged. The support and encouragement of friends, family, and/or even strangers can help, but finally you have to find your reasons for doing it *in doing it*.

◆ Write for the good of the work—as opposed to writing for others or writing for self.

◆ Serve your stories relentlessly by doing everything you can to make them as good as you can make them (e.g., letting others read them, trying to revise them to perfection, carrying out appropriate research instead of trying to fake it).

◆ Write stories you *want* to live with. It isn't always easy to know if a story you're working on will become one you want to live with. You have to write a number of stories that you need to cast off from yourself and not live with. But it's useful to remind yourself that your reason for writing these things is because you want certain stories of your own to live in the world with you.

◆ Write often enough that you miss it if you don't do it. To have a real writing life, you must be writing at least this often. Going to your writing should seem a pleasure rather than a burden to you; if it isn't a pleasure, then you need to shape up your writing life.

◆ Demand of yourself that you grow in your ability, your ambition, your achievement. If you don't feel you're getting somewhere in your writing, then you need to make some changes. Grow or rot, those are your choices. It is one of the happy functions of the writing workshop—the community of your writer-friends—to keep you growing.

These elements of a writers' code are not the secrets to

becoming a writer; they're mere descriptions of a writing life. What is not commonly understood about artists in general and writers in particular is how they find an essential companionship in their work. To the outsider, it can only seem absurd to devote such attention to tedious details, such hours to going over and over manuscripts that any ordinary person would have long ago finished and forgotten, and such intellectual and emotional energy to projects that are as likely to fail as they are to succeed and that in either case promise little or no tangible reward. People who do other things often speak with admiration of the "discipline" required to write, the tone of their voices usually conveying their gratitude that they themselves are not afflicted with such "discipline." But the writer doesn't think in terms of discipline or sacrifice or even risk. The writer desires to write because writing is a lifelong companion with whom it is possible to carry out the most intimate personal exchanges between self and other. Desire for the companionship of writing is the writer's reason for trying to survive.

12 WHAT YOU GET FOR GOOD WRITING

"If you can only learn to write badly enough, you can make an awful lot of money." —Flannery O'Connor
Mystery and Manners

good writing is a calling. Whoever answers it should not do so naively. One of my first "mature" stories, "Poison Oak," went through around 25 drafts to reach its final draft of 28 pages. I composed it on a typewriter; so I typed approximately 700 pages of words to produce the story—at about fifteen minutes a page, or some 175 hours of typing labor. Back then, the going rate for typing was a dollar a page. So if I'd typed all those pages for somebody else, I'd have made $700. Or if I'd typed only the 28 pages of the final draft of the manuscript for somebody else, I'd have made $28. *The New England Review* paid me $25 for "Poison Oak."For all the writing I've published and that I count as "my own work"—eight books counting those forthcoming in 1992, forty stories, a couple hundred poems, and maybe a dozen essays—my pay probably works out to a little more than a dollar an hour. In spite of, or maybe even because of, the lousy pay, I've turned out to be a better writer than I first envisioned myself becoming. A commercial hack is what I first aspired to be.

My quick definition of an artist—someone whose primary aim is to produce original work of the highest quality—suggests high-mindedness, nobility, integrity by choice. But my experience has demonstrated to me that it's much more a matter of inclination than choice. When I encounter unlikely people who happen to be artists, I have to remind myself of what I know quite intimately, that the inclination toward artistry is common, human, and random. It's mostly a matter of dissatisfaction—of feeling vaguely askew with the universe and wanting to construct something— some magical object or talisman—that we hope will correct our cosmic alignment. Then it's a matter of being unable to leave that constructed something alone until we have pestered it into being exactly the way we want it to be. Choosing to be an artist won't help you become one if you're not inclined that way. Choosing not to be an artist may not save you from becoming one if you are inclined that way.

Around the age of nineteen, I was enormously impressed by Herman Wouk's *Youngblood Hawke,* a popular novel based loosely and sensationally on the life of Thomas Wolfe. That book was what set me thinking about trying to become a writer. My education since then has taught me to perceive the inaccuracies in its portrayal of the life of a writer, along with its esthetic failures; even so, I remember *Youngblood Hawke* with a kind of wistful pleasure.

I'd like to write books that lots of people would read and love. If I could write like Stephen King, I'd be sorely tempted to do it; whereas if I could write like Marcel Proust or James Joyce or William Gass or William Gaddis or Guy Davenport, I definitely wouldn't. Given a choice, I expect I'd take the low road.

But blessed or cursed—whichever, it all comes to the same thing—I have no choice but to write like myself.

I write the way I write because that's how the language and I work it out. The act of composition, for me, is a gradual working my way toward a certain way for my writing to be that seems to me *right.* That intuitively-determined "certain way"—down to the length and the tone of my sentences, the number of conjunctions I'll allow myself in a given paragraph, and the way I use dashes— is the truth of things, as I am able to locate it in my stories, poems, or essays.

My personal inclination is to fuss with my writing over a

period of time, to ask my writer pals to criticize it, to try one thing and another, to cut and add and change and combine and separate and move the parts around this way and that way, to revise the piece of writing many times in an effort to move it closer to that "certain way." To work in this tedious manner has also come to feel right to me. Fussing is the method that suits my abilities; I'm not good at fast thinking or off-the-top-of-my-head composing; I need to write a thing over and over again to be able to understand it and to get it right.

Along with fussing, what I write about—my subject matter—is also a basic impulse of my personality. Given crayons and paper, my oldest daughter, at around the age of seven, used to draw elaborate bunny palaces. Given the same materials at the same age, my youngest daughter drew rows of ballerinas. Given language, there are certain patterns I am similarly inclined to pursue—for reasons deeply embedded in my brain and body cells.

From 23 years of commitment to the craft of writing, I've refined my methods of pursuing these patterns of my personality through composing narratives. I'm better able to recognize when I'm on the right track, and when a pattern is emerging in a piece of my writing, I've come to know how to use revision to go further with it, to get deeper into it. Once I have completely grasped it, a pattern loses its value to me, except insofar as it leads to the next one. I can't stay where I am and can't go backwards. Whether I want to or not, I have to keep on moving forward. What I call "my own writing" is what I'm producing when I am pursuing those patterns, seeking to write in that "certain way." Training and luck (a part of which is that I've never made a lot of money with my own writing) have allowed me to give this very personal activity a more and more important place in my daily life. Having done lots of other kinds of writing (some of which *has* paid me well), I've come to understand a clear distinction between that work and the kind that offers me a chance to pursue what W. S. Merwin's speaker in "Lemuel's Blessing" calls "what is essential to me." The difference is one of direction: "other writing" is aimed outward; its target is money, explanation, communication, persuasiveness, something other than the realization of those patterns of an author's personality.

When I'm working on "my own writing," though I rarely pay attention to it, I experience a sense of physical "rightness"—very much like eating when I'm hungry, drinking when I'm thirsty, sleeping when I'm tired: my body's signals are that I'm doing exactly what I ought to be doing. All my other activities of choice fail to give me such a sense of rightness, even the ones I enjoy (such as tennis, volleyball, or croquet), the ones I'm thought to be good at (such as teaching or reading aloud), or the ones that the world would judge to be "appropriate" (such as cooking dinner for my family, watering the houseplants, or writing letters to my distant family-members and friends).

I'd even go so far as to say that my body gives signals of protest about all my other activities of choice. I can be playing my best tennis ever and become aware of my legs' yearning to carry me back to my room, my desk, my computer. I can be engaged in a spirited classroom debate when suddenly I'll feel this trickle of anxious sweat down my ribcage and hear a faint voice way down in some dark corridor of my brain whispering, "Phony! Show-off! Shit-Merchant!"

The most important aspects of "my own writing" are beyond (or beneath or above) my conscious will. I'm not a zombie—at least I hope I'm not, I suppose you never know—and I think I have a general idea about where I'm going when I begin a piece of writing. In terms of the piece I end up producing, that general idea may be entirely correct or all wrong. But the good stuff of my writing, the part that continues to interest me through the years, is what has come unexpectedly—during the actual act of composition—what my intuition rather than my planning has brought onto the page.

Autobiography may be the most direct approach to one's "own writing," but it does not guarantee realization of any pattern, let alone a deep one; sometimes autobiography is just autobiography, a sequence of facts about a life. Sometimes its author may realize a superficial or an imposed pattern. Sometimes the biggest problem with autobiography is that the author knows too much about the subject, so that the known crowds out the possibility of discovering the unknown.

Discovery is the spark that ignites the essential energy of a work of art. When I sit down to write, I don't have a thing to say, not even the beginning of a message, but I usually have a great deal that I have begun to feel the need to find out. When revelation begins to emerge from a poem or story or essay as I'm working on it, that's when I feel the thing taking on its own life.

What do I mean by "discovery" and "finding out something"? Usually the kind of discovery I make is a connection—or maybe an understanding of the connection—between or among certain elements that present themselves in my writing. "Poison Oak" is as good an example as any: it's a story about a young boy's partial understanding of a hired man's dangerous and harmful sexual obsession with his mother. The main insight I gained from writing that story is suggested in the following passage about the dangerous man's replacement:

> I liked [the new hired man] because he was very nice to me,... but I was becoming less and less interested in him. The only time he seemed at all dangerous was when he went into the barn to pray...

Through writing "Poison Oak," I made a connection between my feelings toward two hired men I vividly remembered from my childhood, one diabolical and the other angelic; in the process of writing about characters based on them, I was able to think about these men and how they informed my personality. Therefore, I learned something—or I came to acknowledge something—about my own attraction to the dangerous, the forbidden, and the harmful.

Here are some basic principles I believe about writing and art:

◆ Essential to the making of literary art is the artist's pursuit through writing of the deepest patterns of his or her personality.

◆ The aim of this pursuit for the artist is a written work that embodies significant personal discovery. The artist may pursue those patterns, but if the artist doesn't find out anything in the writing, what he or she produces will lack the crucial energy of art.

◆ Revision is the refining of a piece of writing to such an extent that the discovered pattern yields an exact revelation. Revision is the artist's struggle to achieve a precise understanding of what has been generally discovered in drafting a piece of writing.

◆ Usually what the artist finds out is "hard knowledge," something perhaps unattractive or difficult to accept, e.g., the fact that one is attracted to what is dangerous and harmful.

◆ The discoveries made through writing are liberating to the artist. If they are "hard knowledge," these discoveries nevertheless grant the artist a permanent unburdening. Thus personal liberation is the basic incentive for trying to write as well as one can. Through writing—the process itself must produce the discovery—the literary artist seeks to work through the confining forces of his or her life toward freedom.

My subscription to these principles has emerged from my writing life. They weren't the ideas I had in mind when I began my writing life. What I had in mind then was more in the line of *Youngblood Hawke*, both in terms of the kind of book I wanted to write and in terms of the kind of life I thought I wanted to live. I had in mind work that would come easy to me and for which I would receive a good deal of money and adoration. I did not have in mind typing 700 pages to get a 28-page story. I did not have in mind having to come to terms with unpleasant facts about myself. I had in mind quickly becoming a beloved genius. What I have gotten to be over almost a quarter of a century is a more or less respected writer.

I know that I'm lucky to have gotten what I have. I'm acquainted with more gifted people who've worked harder on their writing than I have and haven't gotten anything.

Here are some of the elements of my luck:

◆ Members of both sides of my family loved books. My parents read aloud to and with my brothers and me. My grandfather was a great story-teller.

◆ From both sides of my family I have inherited patience, powers of concentration, the inclination to work hard and to try to overcome discouragement.

◆ For eighth-grade, freshman, junior, and senior English, Mrs. Arraga Young was my teacher. She gave me a superior understanding of syntax.

◆ As a boy, I had a good deal of training in and experience with music.

◆ I couldn't really "cut it" as an English major at the University of Virginia. Thus I was fortunate enough to flunk out of Virginia and serve in the U. S. Army as an enlisted man in Germany and Vietnam.

◆ My readings of Faulkner, Hemingway, James Baldwin, and others were passionately accomplished outside the classroom. Thus I evaded a good deal of the conventional intellectualization of literature that occurs in the academy.

◆ My early writing teachers at the University of Virginia— John Coleman, James Kraft, and Peter Taylor—encouraged me. Taylor gave me a good look at a man with a writing life and served as a valuable role model of a respected story-writer. When it became evident that I wasn't a Hemingway, a Faulkner, or even a Herman Wouk, I took refuge in what I knew about Peter Taylor's life and his work.

◆ My wife was willing to work to support me and my efforts to write during the first years of our marriage. For almost twenty-four years she has continued to provide emotional support for my writing even though my writing is not always to her liking.

◆ My experience in Vietnam gave me something to write about that was of interest to some editors. Thus, my first two story-publications, in *The Georgia Review* in Fall 1969 and in *Esquire* in January 1971, were stories about Vietnam.

◆ My year of graduate study at Hollins College under the mentorship of George Garrett helped me begin thinking of myself as a writer.

◆ My two years of graduate study at Columbia University helped me understand literary and publishing politics and to see how I could successfully compete with my aspiring-writer peers.

◆ My story in *Esquire* was on the newsstands when I interviewed for a teaching job at the MLA meeting in New York in December 1970. Thus I got a good job at the University of Vermont.

◆ As it turned out, after I got my teaching job (with no teaching experience whatsoever), I did have some ability in the classroom. Thus I have been granted a way of supporting myself other than through what I can make with my writing alone.

Luck has everything to do with an artist's being able to take possession of his or her given work. For one thing, an artist needs a number of years to understand in personal terms how the process of making art works and to establish the working habits that will produce works of art. In my own case, flunking out of the University of Virginia and joining the army gave me three extra years of growing up before I had to graduate; then I was granted an additional three years of graduate study in which writing had first claims on my time, energy, and attention. So I got six "free" years seriously to try to realize my dreams of becoming a writer, to discover my artistic inclinations, and to establish the habits that would enable me to be productive. I also had the benefit of advice and counsel from older writers who knew what I needed. Had I proceeded on track and on schedule, I would have taken my B.A. after four or five years, gone to law school or gotten a job, and forever after, I'd have been trying to squeeze out an hour or two to give my writing—or worse and more likely, when things got bad at the office, I'd have simply daydreamed about giving it all up and running away to become a writer.

If you wish to make art, an obvious necessity is that you give first priority to your artistic work—in spirit and in fact. Why is this case? Because works of art only come out of the artist's wholehearted effort, out of the artist's being able to give the work everything—knowledge, feeling, energy, passion. The artist must be able to give him- or herself to the work again and again, day in and day out. If your family or your job makes first claims on you, you cannot give your whole self to your artistic work, and what you produce is not likely to be satisfactory to you or to others.

Please note that I do not say that the artist must forget or disregard his or her family. The artist builds his or her life on the belief that an hour of writing time is more important than grocery shopping, but in my view it's possible to write for a couple of hours and then do the grocery shopping, possible to try to write well *and* to keep more or less fresh produce in the refrigerator. You may have to pay for these luxuries with sleep or with a lousy social life, but they're nevertheless available.

So what do you get out of such labor and sacrifice? Mostly what you get is the privilege of doing something that makes extreme demands of you, that asks you for everything you've got. If you're lucky enough to be able to give art what it wants, even occasionally, you should bow your head and say thanks. But even though they are little discussed, there are some "social" rewards for good writing.

Aside and apart from matters of employment, I am a person who has chosen to define himself as a writer. If you're more than casually acquainted with me, you have to know that about me. If we're having a conversation, and you don't ask me what I do, I'm likely to tell you anyway. That's how I wish to live in the world, as a person whose main work in life is known to be writing.

That's the surface of my identity. The substance of it is my writing itself, which I have chosen to place out in the world. If you've read two or three of my books, the odds are that you know me better than you know your next-door neighbor. You may even know me better than you know your brother, your father, your husband, your wife, your son or your daughter. I don't mean *know* literally, because even the most autobiographical of my work is filled with so much made-up material that it will not yield a trustworthy factual account of my experience. But you'll know me—there isn't any other way to put this—spiritually: you'll know what is at the center of my personality; you'll know what I think about, what troubles me, what comforts me, what I'm afraid of, what I admire, what I care about, what I hate, what I notice about people, and so on.

Admittedly this is a controlled, an edited, maybe even a contrived, version of myself that my written work puts forth. Since I obviously have the power *not* to publish those works that reveal aspects of myself I don't want to reveal, it's accurate to say that whatever I *have* revealed in my published work has been a matter of deliberate choice. So far as I know, I haven't let anything slip.

Yet it seems to me that in pages any stranger or enemy can easily find and examine in a library, I have revealed everything there is to reveal about myself. I feel that in my published work all my weaknesses of character have been made so evident that balding, duck-footed, and pot-bellied, I stand naked before my reader.

Of course, in the same pages, what can be said in my favor has also been put forth. If my weaknesses are revealed, then so, too, are my strengths—straightforwardly there, not in the form of the self-promotion I might try to hand you if I were applying to you for a job.

In making my narratives, I have pitted these pros and cons of the self against each other. What I have come up with in the finished pieces are the ways I have weighed them out, the ways I have tried to make them balance. On the one hand, in every piece of my writing that I care about, I've engaged in some kind of spiritual struggle. On the other hand, I've simply tried to tell a good story. These two aspects of my writing process—the high-minded and the trashy—are inseparable.

Perhaps the basic discoveries of my writing life have been that in order to tell a good story, I have to carry out a spiritual struggle and that making narratives is my method of spiritual inquiry. If I'd had my choice years ago, I'd have picked another approach to writing—namely the quick and easy. In this regard, I've taken comfort from these lines from Franz Kafka's "The Hunger Artist": "...I couldn't find the food I liked. If I had found it, believe me, I should have made no fuss and stuffed myself like you or anyone else."

A valuable by-product of the way I have been forced to write— or the one way that I have discovered it to be possible for me to write—is that I live in the world as a known person. I'm not talking about fame or reputation here; I'm talking about the fact that my spiritual checkbook is out there in the open for you or anybody else to have a look at. My work enables me to examine my life, and the struggles of that examination are a matter of public record. People who associate with me know the most important things there are to know about me. I can be "straight" with the world.

Difficulties go with making oneself so available. In the process of reckoning with oneself, one can hurt family members and friends, who might not wish to be revealed to the world or who might prefer to reveal themselves in their own terms. Instead of love and admiration, one can win anger and alienation. One can show oneself to be stupid, obtuse, insensitive, ignorant, treacherous, and generally despicable. And one can't take it back.

This ongoing nakedness, in my opinion, is one reason why some very fine writers get nervous, defensive, and sometimes pretty tricky about discussing their own work. We admire their writing so much we can't imagine why they'd feel weird talking about it. But it's one thing to walk around naked in a world where most people are very well dressed; most of the time, nobody says anything about it, and you can pretend that you're just like everybody else. It's something else when you're called upon to try to account for why you choose to live this way; that's when you begin to seem a little freakish to yourself.

In spite of these liabilities, it seems to me that living in the world as a known person is a privilege. It is perhaps the ultimate incentive for trying to practice an art form. The opposite circumstance, living within reticence or a permanent disguise, must be a severe form of suffering.

A teasing game sometimes played by German parents and their young children goes this way: though the child may be in the immediate presence of the parent, the parent nevertheless calls out, *Wo bist du?*—Where are you?—and the child responds, *Ich bin hier!*—I am here! This ritual is repeated until the parent finally gives in to the child's insistence that it is in fact *hier*. The world constantly whispers this same question to us, "Where are you?" and our lives are our answers: "I am here." Lots of times my answer has had to be, "I don't know where the hell I am," or "Maybe I'm over here," or "I hope this is me here."

My best answer, though, is my written work, and it probably

goes something like this: "It may not be much, but at least I'm here by the page and a half that I wrote this morning. I am here in this poem. I set down a word and then another beside it. I am here." By virtue of writing the way I write and therefore living in the world as a known person, I am granted above-average metaphysical certainty.

In less pretentious terms, if trying to write the best you can is what is most important to you, your pay may be lousy, your family may have disowned you, your enemies may be suing you, your agent may not be returning your calls, your editor may have been fired, your friends may be ready to do serious harm to you, and the lettuce in your refrigerator may be turning brown and mushy around the edges, but for better or for worse, you've taken possession of your life.

UNIVERSITY PRESS OF NEW ENGLAND publishes books under its own imprint and is the publisher for Brandeis University Press, Dartmouth College, Middlebury College Press, University of New Hampshire, Tufts University, and Wesleyan University Press.

LIBRARY OF CONGRESS CATALOGING-IN-PUBLICATION DATA
Huddle, David, 1942–
      The writing habit / David Huddle.
          p.   cm.
          ISBN 0–87451–668–4
          1. Authorship.   I. Title.
PN151.H78   1994
808'.02—dc20   93–38327
   ∞   CIP